MOTIVATE FROM WITHIN

MOTIVATE FROM
WITHIN

A YOUNG ADULT'S GUIDE TO
SHOOTING FOR THE STARS

CAMILLE ADANA

CREATOR OF

This book contains true stories provided by young people, all of which are used with written permission. Stories have been condensed and edited for clarity, and some details have been changed to ensure anonymity.

Co-written by Sheila Ashdown
Cover design by Dana Csakany
Interior design by Jennifer Omner
Author photo by Angie Tabaczynski

ISBN: 978-0-9961926-0-6
Library of Congress Control Number: 2015904795

Visit ADANA Dynamics online at www.adanadynamics.com to view a photo gallery, stay in touch with Camille, and share your own stories.

Dedicated to the memory of Alex Rovello
Cleveland High School (Portland, Oregon)
Class of 2010

Alex, you were the epitome of a young adult who shot for the stars. Thank you for being motivated from within. You affected my life immensely and will never be forgotten.

CONTENTS

FOREWORD

Dear Reader,

If you haven't had the pleasure of meeting this dynamic, endearing person, then you haven't had the opportunity of an encounter that leaves every person feeling more significant than before. Camille genuinely makes the people around her happier for just being themselves, which in turn increases their own capacities for goodness.

Camille came into my life one August morning, walking through the gym doors in her first days of high school. Everyone she interacted with did nothing but smile or laugh. Her tremendous need for information, her work ethic, and her desire to improve in everything she did made her such a unique and inspiring person to teach and coach. Throughout the years, her ability to connect with every person she met, no matter what their differences were, opened a social path of opportunity like no other.

As a teacher—and now an author—Camille excels in her ability to gain the trust and respect of her students and readers, with her real-life inspirational talks and innovative lessons. Most amazing is her talent and skill in empowering young people to take control of their own lives. It's clear that she's making a huge difference as a teacher, coach, and mentor of young people. Because Camille speaks her truth, her loyalty, life experience, and genuine heart just adds more admirers to her already long list.

I'm sincerely thankful that, with this book, Camille is sharing her capacity for making the world a better place.

Linda McLellan
Teacher of physical education and health
Benson High School
Portland, Oregon

LETTER TO PARENTS, GUARDIANS, EDUCATORS, COACHES, AND ROLE MODELS

We all want the same for our kids and teenagers. We want them to have confidence and aspirations, to make good choices, and to ultimately grow into healthy, independent adults.

To help young people shoot for the stars, we adults have to be fully developed. Even though we're human and we have our flaws and challenges, we're in the spotlight. We have to be the best versions of ourselves, because young people are watching us to learn how to be adults. We need to help them, not hinder them. We all have so many kids and young adults that we're dealing with, and they're all having their unique experience in our classes, on our teams, and within our households. At home, parents have to guide their kids through some really tough circumstances, whether that's divorce, illness, death of a loved one, financial difficulties, or body image issues. As educators, we need to understand the emotional landscape of ourselves and our students. As coaches, we need to learn how to be on the same page with our teams. We have to know our athletes' wants, needs, and expectations if we're going to help them succeed.

Motivate from Within gives us framework and a common language for addressing all of these issues. In the book, I introduce ADANA Dynamics, a success process that inspires readers of all ages to deal with their past, aspire to the future, and create a life they're proud of. ADANA Dynamics has five parts, each building upon the other:

A: Acknowledge Your Current Reality
D: Deal with Yesterday
A: Aspire for Tomorrow
N: No-Nonsense Approach
A: Accountability

This step-by-step process is not strictly for teenagers or early adolescents. The ADANA Dynamics have always been a process I've used to grow through the hard, confusing times that we experience as humans, no matter our age or stage or life. I encourage you to use this approach for yourself. The more we look within, the more dynamic of a role we can play in others' lives. It also doesn't hurt for us to feel the improvement and exhilaration in our own lives.

HOW TO USE THIS BOOK AS A PARENT, GUARDIAN, EDUCATOR, COACH, OR ROLE MODEL

- **Read the book.** That way, you can know what your young adults and students are involved in and thinking about, and you can help them in that process.
- **Try the "Do Now" Exercises.** These exercises are designed to create shifting experiences. Try them and feel the difference in your own life. It might even stir up your creative juices to come up with your own hands-on learning experiences to do with your kids and students. Go for it. Be creative and have fun with it.
- **Allow the kids and young adults in your life to acknowledge their current reality.** This can be hard, because your child, student, or athlete might be experiencing a difficulty that relates to you, or is caused by your flaws or inconsistencies. You're human. That's okay. This book isn't designed to throw you under the bus. However, I encourage you to really hear them and acknowledge what they're saying. Even if you're tempted to think their teenage problems are silly, take them seriously. Even if you don't agree with their aspirations, respect them as individuals. This will cultivate a mutually respectful relationship.
- **Have candid conversations.** Be a compassionate listener and get to know your kids, students, and athletes for who they are, not who you expect them to be. Don't be afraid to level with them. Get down and dirty with it. Real communication is candid.

I truly believe that a positive reciprocal relationship can exist between adults and young people. My hope is that every child, teenager, twenty-something, and adult who reads *Motivate from Within* will take something of value from the ADANA Dynamics process. When motivated people influence other motivated people, success multiplies.

Love,

Camille Adana

Creator of ADANA Dynamics

INTRODUCTION

START FROM THE HEART
AND SHOOT FOR THE STARS

We all go through hardship and challenges. But we all have the innate capacity to succeed in spite of them. It's not easy—for any of us. I've been teaching for sixteen years, and have had more than twenty thousand high school students cross my path. Even as teenagers, they deal with major life issues: conflict at home, financial hardship, low self-esteem, heartbreak, learning difficulties, physical or mental illness, and much more. Popular culture tells us that childhood should be easy and carefree. But I can tell you from experience: just because you're young, you're not immune to hardship. Life is a long education in learning to work through it.

Jack Canfield, bestselling author of *The Success Principles* and *Dare to Win*, says that "knowing how to achieve success is like knowing the combination to a lock. If you are missing any of the numbers, or have them in the wrong order, the lock won't open."

When I look at those students who succeed in spite of life's many challenges, it's because they've found the numbers to their own personal combination lock. They look within their heart to cultivate self-esteem and healthy priorities. They dream big, define success for themselves, and then go after it with a positive attitude and forward thinking. The people who *don't* succeed? They're the ones who are trapped in the past and tangled up in the petty dramas of the moment. They don't make goals, because they're too busy making excuses. They're spinning away on that combination lock, working on the wrong numbers, and they're not making much progress.

What if I asked you to think of one thing you want from life? What would it be? You want to be a rock star? You want to get married and have kids? You want to be a millionaire? Okay. Good. It's healthy to have big dreams. I want you to shoot for the stars. But you're only going to get what you want if you foster a burning desire in your heart and then you take the practical steps to make it happen. Big dreams take big work. This book will help you on that journey. I've included inspiring concepts, personal stories, and hands-on exercises that are designed to help you set goals and achieve them.

TAKE IT FROM ME—I'VE BEEN THERE

I've experienced just about every hardship you can imagine, starting from the day I was born. I was premature, weighing only 3 pounds and 9 ounces. I fought for my life without even knowing it, and have been fighting ever since.

This drive, this internal motivation, got me through a childhood filled with almost every imaginable challenge. I grew up in a dirt poor family, with parents who were drug- and alcohol-addicted. My father was physically and emotionally violent. I had learning difficulties and missed major pieces of my early education because we were constantly getting evicted and moving from place to place. I was sexually abused. I've had health problems. I've experienced racism as the blond-haired, light-skinned daughter of a Filipino man. I've had depression and suicidal thoughts.

However, these circumstances didn't break me. I wanted a better life for myself, and I had a lot of intrinsic motivation to go after it. But I also had great forces of external motivation. I'm blessed that I had phenomenal people in my world—teachers, coaches, and role models—who gave me an outside perspective and inspired me to aspire. I went on to have a successful career as a high school and college athlete, which included a full-ride scholarship to college. As an athlete, I was voted 18 times to be the most inspirational player on the team. After college, I went on to a 16-year (and counting) career in education, teaching physical education, health, and leadership, and coaching volleyball, basketball, and softball. It was those early mentors and role models who inspired me to become a teacher. It's my way of giving back and paying it forward. And now, with this book, I want to motivate you—just as those teachers, coaches, and role models motivated and supported me during a time when I really needed it.

Sometimes I'm amazed that I'm here—writing this motivational book from the perspective of a healthy, happy adult. People who don't know my history are shocked when they find out. Why are they shocked? Because most people let hardship keep them down their whole lives. Not me. I'm living proof that you can overcome your past and create a fulfilling future for yourself. You've got your own story, your own traumas and dramas. We all do. But I'm here to tell you: Don't give up on yourself.

I'm a candid person, and throughout this book I share details of my personal story to help illuminate the philosophy and strategies that have allowed me to thrive. I'm grateful for my past, and I share it with you in hopes that, one day, you too will be grateful for your past.

ADANA DYNAMICS: GIVING YOU THE TOOLS TO LIVE YOUR BEST LIFE

In this book, you'll be introduced to ADANA Dynamics, five principles of personal development that will help you create major shifts in your life. By actively engaging with the ADANA process, you'll gain insights and tools to be your best self and live your best life. The acronym "ADANA" corresponds to each of the five steps of the process:

A: ACKNOWLEDGE YOUR CURRENT REALITY

Acknowledging your current reality means looking closely at yourself and taking an honest inventory of all domains of life, which I like to call the Six Fs: Future (academics, career), Fitness (including nutrition), Friendships (including romantic relationships), Family, Finances, and Fun (hobbies). Only after you dig deep and do a self-assessment can you move forward. You have to first open your eyes and really dissect those past experiences—hardships, limiting mindsets, bad habits—that routinely hold you back. Then you can take the next step...

D: DEAL WITH YESTERDAY

When you deal with yesterday, you cleanse yourself of your past and ready yourself to move toward a better future. I truly feel that when a person cleans up the past, personal transformation is inevitable. "Dealing with it" is a very active and highly personalized part of the ADANA Dynamics process. You'll experience major shifts in mindset and explore healthy ways to cope—emotionally, mentally, and physically.

A: ASPIRE FOR TOMORROW

After you create a clean slate by acknowledging your reality and dealing with it, you're ready to create the life of your dreams. This is where it gets fun. When you aspire, you jumpstart your future. This means dreaming big, setting small and big goals, getting in touch with what *you* want from life, and surrounding yourself with the role models and mentors who can help you get it.

N: NO-NONSENSE APPROACH

A no-nonsense approach means being both loving *and* honest with yourself—and surrounding yourself with others who will do the same. This book is designed to bust you into gear and encourage you to push yourself. You've got one life, and I want you to live it! Go get it! Love it! But in order to do so, you've got to put away the flimsy excuses and become a badass. That's the no-nonsense approach to living a life you'll love.

A: ACCOUNTABILITY

Holding yourself accountable means taking 100 percent responsibility for your life. Once you decide to go after your aspirations, you have to learn to hold yourself accountable to truly following through. We'll talk about cultivating an internal sense of commitment as well as surrounding yourself with accountability partners who can help keep you on track.

· · ·

How do I know that ADANA Dynamics works? Because I use it myself, and I use it in my classroom and with my athletes. I've witnessed the ways it has truly shifted the lives of those who have learned the approach, fallen in love with it, and followed through on using it in their daily lives. These are principles that you can use and build on throughout your entire life. Learn it now, practice it, and it'll become second nature for you. Challenges and hardships come in many forms, and these tools and mindsets are versatile enough to get you through anything that comes at you. You have one precious life, and you owe it to yourself to envision the great possibilities and set your mind and heart to going after them. ADANA Dynamics will help you do just that.

HOW TO USE THIS BOOK

The ADANA Dynamics approach is all about giving you the tools so that you can motivate from within. No one can do it for you. The only way you're going to move forward is with intrinsic motivation—in other words, motivation that comes from *inside of you*. ADANA Dynamics is a life-changing system that can help you shift your life in major ways. But it can't happen all at once. Life is a long path of personal development. Have compassion for where you're at right now, while also pressing forward and challenging yourself.

If you read this book carefully and allow it to sink in, you're going to take something away from it. You might read a chapter that really shifts you, and another that doesn't resonate with you and your experiences. That's okay. We're all different, and the steps I've taken might be different from the steps you need to take. Personal development is an individual practice. Experiment and see what works for you.

There are some books that speak to you right now, and others that need some time. You won't take it *all* in—that's just not possible—but take what you can use right now. When you're ready, revisit the book. When you reread a book at different points in your life, you get something new out of it. Keep this one on your shelf and refer back to it.

DO NOW! DON'T WAIT ANOTHER MINUTE TO MAKE YOUR LIFE BETTER

There's a proverb that says, "The best time to plant a tree was twenty years ago. The second best time is now." How does that apply to your personal development? What it means is, when you look at your current reality, there are two options: you can be disappointed that the past didn't go differently, or you can do something about it right now. Not yesterday. Not tomorrow. NOW.

This book includes "Do Now" exercises that give you hands-on opportunities to create life-altering moments for yourself. You can't just read about changing your life—you have to try it for yourself. The "Do Now" exercises include journaling, meditation, table talk, letter writing, and visionary exercises. These are activities that you can repeat over and over to get new and deeper results every time. I highly recommend having a journal or dedicated notebook on hand when you read *Motivate from Within* so that you can take notes and capture the feelings and "aha" moments as they arise. When you experience a shift, you'll know it. You'll get butterflies in your stomach, your palms will sweat, you'll get excited. It's a little like falling in love—in love with life and all of its possibilities.

I encourage you to set aside time in your life to perform the "Do Now" exercises. Personal development requires action. These actions are the seeds of your success. If you start right now, you'll be able to look back in twenty years and think "I'm so glad I planted that tree."

At the back of the book, you'll find a complete list of the "Do Now" exercises. Revisit the list as often as you can and look for ways to apply to the activities to your life.

DON'T JUST TAKE MY WORD FOR IT...

As a high school teacher and coach, I'm fortunate to be surrounded every day by insightful young adults with experiences that you can relate to. I've included some of their stories here, in their own words. When young adults tell their stories in my classroom, when they make themselves vulnerable, the level of empathy improves between students. At the same time, when students experience the openness and respect of their peers, their personal, internal dialogue becomes more focused and positive. It's amazing to witness. And though the details of their lives may differ from your own, at the heart of it, they're not so different from you. Human beings have similar struggles, and when we share our stories, we're able to find comfort and perspective and know that we've got friends in this world.

PART 1

ACKNOWLEDGE YOUR CURRENT REALITY

The present moment is all we really have. The past is done and gone, and the future has yet to be created. But though we can't change where we've come from, we *can* make choices and take actions *right now* that will set us on the path toward the future of our dreams.

In order to get to right now, we have to go back to the past and acknowledge the influential, defining moments that are playing a major role in our life today. We are who we are because of yesterday. But we can't go forward if we're focused on the past. The past stagnates, the future motivates. So we have to say goodbye to yesterday in order to feel good about the present and set goals for the future.

When you acknowledge your current reality, you take stock of everything that has affected you until now, in all of the Six Fs: Future, Fitness, Friendships, Family, Finances, and Fun. Of course, you're a unique individual, and your current reality is completely different from anyone else's, but it likely includes aspects such as...

- Family dynamics and parental expectations
- Academics and extracurriculars
- Love and relationships
- Sexuality and gender
- Spirituality and religion
- Personal identity and self-esteem
- Physical health and relationship with food
- Drug and alcohol use

Acknowledging your current reality usually isn't fun, because it brings you face-to-face with difficult feelings. Even happy moments from the past have a way of bringing up sadness in the present. But I know from experience that there's nothing you can't get over. You *can* process and disconnect from that past energy and heal yourself from the traumatic experiences and pain that led up to today. Acknowledging your current reality is an important first step on the journey of personal development.

To start, we'll explore ways to connect with your emotions, love yourself, analyze the influences in your life, see the greatness in everyone (including you!), and cultivate the belief that everything happens for a reason. We're talking about shifting your mindset in a major way. Get ready!

FEEL YOUR FEELINGS

Acknowledging your reality can be difficult. When you lay all your hardships and challenges out in front of you, it *will* bring up difficult emotions. Sadness, fear, anger, hopelessness. You might be tempted to push those feelings away because they're unpleasant. But as with so much in life, the only way out is through. If you try to ignore or squash your emotions, they'll only be manifested in other ways. Unprocessed emotions can have a seriously detrimental effect on your physical health, your emotional well-being, and your relationships with family and friends. And if you hold on to a negative emotion for *too* long, you're in danger of forming that emotion into a habit or an identity. We do not want to be defined and ruled by sadness, pain, or anger. We are all so much more than that, and capable of so much more than that.

Connecting to your feelings is a good first step on a journey of personal development. You have to connect to feelings before you can move anywhere else.

FIND TIME TO SIT WITH YOUR EMOTIONS

When I was a little girl, I got in the practice of crying at night when I was alone in my bedroom. This was the time that I took for myself to sit with my feelings and process my daily pain. I was enmeshed in a scary, dysfunctional home environment, but when I was alone at night, I felt safe. During the day, I had to carefully guard my emotions. At school, I hid the awful reality of my home life from my teachers and classmates. And when I got home, I was forced to tiptoe around my parents' volatile behavior while protecting my two young siblings. It was only at night that I could finally be alone and really let my feelings out. Starting at the age of five, I would reflect on my day—the reality of my life, the good and the bad—and I would let it out in cleansing tears. For me, this wasn't a sad process; it gave me space to feel and heal. I would cry myself to sleep and then wake up the next day, excited to get to school because it was such a wonderful escape. In a way, it let me hit the "reset" button on my life so that I could leave one day behind and try to make the best of the next one.

Part of why it's so important to sit and examine your feelings is that, if you don't, the feelings don't go away—they simply manifest in other ways. My younger brother, Robert, was very angry growing up. Where I cried, Robert fought. He masked his own pain by taking it out on himself and others. It was his only way of expressing himself. If Robert cried, our dad would slap him and push him around, all the while telling him to get tough. He encouraged my brother to be macho and rebellious. Sadness definitely wasn't part of the program. As a kid, Robert didn't know he could make a different choice. Why? Because nobody told him. And unlike me, he wasn't in the habit of taking the time to reflect and process.

Luckily, my brother is a natural optimist, so once he was away from our family influence, he was able to recover and let go of a lot of that anger that was so destructive to him when he was young. But other people aren't so fortunate. Many are in danger of simply taking those unexamined emotions and carrying them through life. Some even start to identify *as* that emotion. Instead of experiencing anger or sadness as a temporary and completely natural part of the human experience, they create an identity as an "angry person" or "sad person." How incredibly limited is that? It doesn't have to be this way. But if you want to gain the skills in processing your emotions, you have to make time to sit with them.

DO NOW! MEDITATE TO DISCOVER YOUR FEELINGS

Find a quiet space where you won't be interrupted. Sit comfortably and take a few slow, deep breaths, in and out. When you're ready, tune into your body. What are you feeling right now? There's no need to judge the feeling or try to change it—simply recognize it for what it is. Where in your body does that feeling reside? Is it in your gut, your chest, your head? This is an act of self-discovery. Sit for five to ten minutes, or until you feel ready to end the meditation.

DON'T NEGLECT THE GOOD FEELINGS

We have a whole spectrum of emotions to choose from. But it's easier to focus on the negative. When you're upset or scared or anxious, those difficult emotions can overshadow the rest. That's natural. In fact, as humans, we have a "negativity bias," which means we're wired to pay more attention to the bad, scary, or dangerous elements of life. As neuropsychologist Rick Hanson says in his book *Hardwiring Happiness*, our brains are "like Velcro for bad experiences but Teflon for good ones." We hold on to those bad experiences while, unfortunately, letting the good ones roll right off.

So, because of your brain's natural inclination toward the negative, it takes more work to focus on the positives. But, when you do, you train your mind and heart to see the good in people and situations. That creates a habit of happiness. The more you practice, the easier it is to make happiness a regular part of your life. When you experience a good feeling, don't push it away or diminish it. Let it in. Embrace the beauty in front of you. Maybe it's a person who loves and supports you. Or a talent or skill that you've worked hard to develop. Or something out in nature—a colorful sunset or a fresh snowfall. See the good and really let it in. Feel it.

I'M FEELING MY FEELINGS…NOW WHAT?

Later in the book, we'll talk strategies for letting go of emotions. But for now, I want you to concentrate on simply connecting with yourself and observing the feelings that arise within you. Managing and coping with emotions are two big components of successful self-development, but you can't effectively manage them until you know what they are.

YOUNG ADULTS TALK ABOUT...WHAT HELPS THEM FEEL THEIR FEELINGS

"When I'm sad or mad, I turn my music up all the way and belt out the lyrics to songs about heartbreak or anger."

"I cry a lot. I'm not ashamed of my tears. I feel so much better when I cry really hard."

DO NOW! FREE WRITE TO DISCOVER YOUR FEELINGS

Grab your journal or a piece of paper. Think about a situation you're going through. Now, without stopping yourself or judging yourself, write down everything you're feeling, with as much depth as you care to go into. You might find that this current situation brings up old feelings about a past situation. That's okay. When you're done, read back through and circle all of the emotion words—"happy," "disappointed," "mad," and so on. In doing so, you can begin to identify where you're spending your time on the emotional spectrum. What this shows you is whether you're allowing yourself to stay in an emotional funk for way too long, or if you're simply just allowing. Allowing is great—just make sure you don't slip into wallowing in an unhealthy place.

CULTIVATE SELF-LOVE

Loving yourself is THE most important choice you can make in life. It is the single most empowering action that you can take—and it's the basis for all other healthy choices. It has to start with self-love.

What does it mean to really love yourself? Well, it's a complex question. We're all on that journey and there's no easy answer. But if you look within yourself, you can find evidence of your love and self-esteem. Check out the list below. These are just a few of the ways you can show love for yourself. Do you answer "yes" to any of these questions?

- Do you look below the surface and value yourself as a whole person?
- Do you eat healthy food?
- Do you exercise regularly?
- Are you picky about who you spend time with, and refuse to settle for low-quality friendships?
- Do you think about your future? Do you have healthy priorities?
- When you make a bad decision, do you take time to reflect and commit to making better ones?
- Do you take your academics seriously? Do you study hard?
- Do you challenge yourself?
- Do you spend quality time with yourself to reflect and recharge?
- Are you compassionate with yourself?

Hopefully, you answered one or more of these questions with a big, loud "YES!" If so, congratulations—you've got the foundations for healthy self-love. Now, that doesn't mean you're never going to get down on yourself. It's natural to have moments of low self-esteem. We all do, and that's okay. In this chapter, we'll explore ways to cultivate true self-love that goes deep and can't be shaken by the daily ups and downs.

SPEND QUALITY TIME WITH YOURSELF

To love yourself, you have to know yourself. And to know yourself, you have to spend quality time with yourself. Don't wait. This is a crucial component of healthy personal development. Spend quality time with yourself *now* to pave a better, easier path later in life.

What is quality time? It could mean spending time by yourself, whether that's journaling or reflecting or meditating—just being with yourself in a quiet way that allows for self-knowledge to arise. Reflection increases your ability to live with intention. When you approach life from a reflective place, you're less opinionated, reactive, and judgmental. When you meet people who are prone to knee-jerk reactions, it's likely that they're in overdrive and craving some personal time that they don't have—or haven't carved out—for themselves.

YOUNG ADULTS TALK ABOUT...WHAT THEY LOVE ABOUT THEMSELVES

"I love that I'm so ambitious. When I set my mind to something, there is nothing stopping me from going after it. I set high goals and refuse to limit myself to what others say is best for me. I know what I want, and I know what I need, and I go after it."

"I am one of the strongest people I know. It took me a long time to realize that, but I am so incredibly strong and dedicated to my well-being."

"I love that I don't care what other people think of me. I don't try to change myself for other people. I will express myself however I want, other people be damned."

"I am smart and capable of making my own decisions."

GOOD CHOICES: THE UPWARD SPIRAL TOWARD SELF-LOVE

One of the best ways to cultivate good self-love is to make good choices. When faced with one of life's many decisions, you can take the life-affirming path. Choose growth. Say YES to your passions. Say YES to your health. Think forward to the future consequences and make your decisions based on what is going to feed your body and soul and propel you toward being the greatest human being you can be. Every time you make a good choice, you cultivate more self-love, which will inspire you to make *more* good choices. It's an upward spiral.

Do you feel like you have a long way to go? That's okay. One of the greatest joys and challenges of personal development is to *love where you're at, but also love the growth process*. Celebrate the successes you're having right now, while also maintaining momentum toward your goals. Sure, there are going to be some interruptions along the way, but if you have a clear goal of what you want for yourself in all of the Six Fs (Future, Fitness, Friendships, Family, Finances, and Fun), you'll continue to make the good choices that will get you there.

DO NOW! WRITE YOURSELF A LOVE LETTER

You have to fall in love with yourself in order to get through this journey of life. Who among us wouldn't like to receive a love letter? Why not send one to yourself? I even took the challenge myself and wrote a love letter to myself. It might feel a bit awkward at first, but give it a try.

Dear Camille,

What I love most about you is your heart. You're not perfect, but you do know that giving your heart daily puts you in a place that feels near perfect. You live your life strictly for love, and it shows up in how you treat yourself and others. I love that you actually, truly, really love yourself and *all* of the people in your life. They may not even know or realize how much, but you love them anyway.

I am totally excited that you're a goal-setter. You're forward thinking, and you're great at visualizing your dreams and making them come true. You've lived a beautiful, fulfilling life so far, and you only want to continue igniting your future so that you can achieve as much personal success as possible. I really love that you've embraced and accepted role models that have changed your life for the better. All the inspirational, motivational people that you respect have literally changed your life, and I love that you actually take in what is being taught and find a way to use the messages in your day-to-day life.

Last but not least, I love you, Camille, for being you. You are unique, and you're oftentimes called "weird" for being so analytical and voicing your thoughts. I love that you lead by example and are comfortable in your skin. I really appreciate how honest, candid, loving, and genuine you are. It's pretty cool that you don't waver in being who you truly are. I hope you continue to lead by example in this way so that everyone who crosses your path feels safe being the unique individual they are.

Much love to you forever and ever,
Camille

A SELF-CONFIDENCE LETTER WRITTEN BY A YOUNG ADULT

Dear You,

My biggest piece of advice for you is to cancel out your negative self-talk and skyrocket your confidence. You can literally accomplish any goal and do anything you want to if you just let yourself go. Confidence is key. Just look at the times in basketball games or social situations when you went in with confidence and self-esteem. You had the most fun and performed best when you decided to leave your nerves behind and not let them affect what you really wanted to do. Basically, tell your mind to fuck off when it's feeding you all the bullshit it does. *I don't work hard. I can't reach that goal; it's impossible. You are so awkward. These people don't like you. I'll mess up.* These depressing phrases that always repeat in your head are complete bullshit and you can block them out. Don't let yourself fall short of your dreams because you are following the standards of what others think is realistic or reachable. Embody the mindset of someone like Ferris Bueller, who is badass and carefree. Right now I will prove to you that your negative self-talk is bullshit and why you should be the most confident person in the world.

Get your swagger back, man. You can still be the basketball player you aspire to be. Don't let your knee problems and surgery make you think you can't anymore. You have worked your ass off all your life and don't let these roadblocks take that away from you. All it does is make you more battle-tested. So there is no need to be nervous about playing high school basketball. This is the fun part. When your mind tells you that you don't work hard, just remember all the times others pointed out your great work ethic, and recount times you yourself noticed how hard you were working. You worked hard before your surgery, you worked hard to get back, and you are working hard now. And I have full confidence that you will take it to the next level and execute your workout plans. If you do that, and play the way you know you can, where you don't overthink, you can accomplish every goal you establish. You have put in the work and will continue to put in the work. Be happy with yourself. You deserve success.

You continue to overcome countless hardships in your life. From your mom's brain injury to your knee surgery you did not let it get you down. You have kept a 4.0 GPA your whole life, even when you had to take 3 hour trips to the hospital everyday while doing physical therapy. Every time you are worried about getting schoolwork done, you always get it done, no matter the bind you were in. So don't worry or overstress. Enjoy yourself. You possess the talent and the work ethic to follow your dream of being an ESPN commentator and SportsCenter anchor.

Don't decide not to chase the jobs because they are two of the hardest professions in the world to get. You possess the passion, ability, and sports-sense to get there. People you trust and strangers have told you the same. If others believe it, believe it yourself.

You are a hard worker, you do deserve success, and you will achieve your goals. Be confident, be full of swagger, and let it go. You are a badass.

Sincerely,

Yourself

FACE IT—DON'T MAKE EXCUSES

To make real change, each and every one of us has to face ourselves. Literally. When I was in high school, trapped in a home life of hardship and violence, I would sit in front of my mirror. I would look at myself and think, "That's Camille. And that has nothing to do with my mom and dad. Or the fact that we're poor. Or that everyone parties and I don't." I knew that I was a separate person, totally responsible for myself and my destiny.

Facing yourself is a powerful act. When you own up to who you really are—separate from the hard circumstances of your life; separate from your family and friends—you get to see yourself as independent and in control of your own future. You can feel good about the parts of yourself that are great. Are you strong? Smart? Kind? Acknowledge that about yourself.

The hard part, though, is that you also have to be 100 percent accountable to yourself. That's a huge responsibility. When I faced myself in the mirror, I realized I couldn't make any excuses. I could've told myself that it was okay to drink alcohol because everyone in my family did. But I knew in my heart that it would just be an excuse. Instead, I decided not to run away from stuff. I acknowledged what was happening in my life, for better or worse, and I knew it was up to me to go after my dreams.

When you face yourself, you *are* going to face challenges. Because, though it's important to acknowledge your strengths, you're also going to come up against your flaws and shortcomings. That's okay. We all have them. That just means it's time to be real with yourself and reach out for the help you need. If you're performing poorly in class or at work, really ask yourself what the problem is. Face it. How can you reach out to make the situation better? Who can you turn to and say, "I'm having a hard time. Can you help me?" This way, instead of making excuses, you empower yourself by reaching out for help and bettering yourself.

For me, when I was a child and then a teenager, I knew that the help I needed was in the form of mentorship. I simply didn't have healthy adult role models at home. My parents were extremely loving, but they were trapped in the dysfunctional cycles they'd been raised within. They were victims of their own hard circumstances, and I needed another way to look at life. So I turned instead to the coaches and teachers in my life. They modeled success for me, and it helped me create a vision for what my own life could be.

Ultimately, you have to fight for yourself. Whatever your strengths, whatever your weaknesses, whatever your circumstances—face them. And then ask yourself, who in your life can you turn to for help?

YOUNG ADULTS TALK ABOUT...FACING IT

"My biggest obstacle is my own procrastination. I can want something as much as I like, but I need the motivation to do it."

"I am very hard on myself, so I am often my own worst enemy."

"I have drama and unnecessary problems in my life."

"I need to be more confident and productive and go after what I want. I need to not be afraid or let my dreams pass me by because I have doubts in myself."

"This sounds cliché, but my biggest obstacle in my life is myself. Everything about me revolves around my being and mind. I control how I think, what I do, how motivated I am, the changes I make, and how I feel."

"A big obstacle in my life is me. I'm reluctant to do anything I'm not comfortable with, and I'm afraid of failing and disappointing anyone."

DO NOW! LOOK IN THE MIRROR

Find a quiet place where you can be alone. Put aside any distractions like your phone, computer, music, or television. Find a comfortable seat in front of a mirror. Look into your eyes and really study yourself. Think about the Six Fs (Future, Fitness, Friendships, Family, Finances, and Fun) and honestly analyze your reality in each of these domains. This is just you versus you. No one else is watching. Give yourself permission to let go of your ego and excuses and just be raw.

You should look in the mirror for at least thirty minutes, but don't feel like you need to put a time limit on this exercise. This experience is very shifting if you don't rush it. Feel your feelings if anything comes up for you. This is a perfect time to forgive yourself for past actions and to visualize what you can change about yourself for the future.

ANALYZE YOUR INFLUENCES

Relationships are an influential part of life, and the early relationships we have—especially with our parents, grandparents, and siblings—have a lifelong impact. We oftentimes repeat our familial patterns without even realizing that we're doing so. If your family is healthy, that's great! That's the ideal. But if your family has a dysfunctional dynamic, that's a problem. Dysfunction has many faces. In some cases, it's obvious—substance abuse, violence, financial distress. In other cases, dysfunction is harder to detect; perhaps you come from a family with poor communication or too-high expectations. In any case, if your home life includes dysfunction or hardship at any level, it can be all too easy to repeat the same patterns in your life. Bad habits learned at home have a way of showing up in our relationships with friends, sweethearts, classmates, and coworkers.

The reality is, even though you didn't choose to be born into dysfunction or hardship, you're the only one who *can* choose to break free. No one can set you free—it's something you must take for yourself. Fortunately, *you can do it*. In this chapter, we explore why and how to analyze the influential people in your life.

WHAT DOES IT MEAN TO ANALYZE YOUR INFLUENCES?

When you analyze your influences, you reflect on the people around you—family, friends, sweethearts, teachers, and so on—in order to see their positive and negative traits. This requires that you step back and try to see people for who they really are. You don't need to be judgmental or harsh about it, but you do need to be realistic. For example, look at your best friend. Undoubtedly he or she has some awesome qualities, or they wouldn't be your best friend. But maybe that person has a quick temper. Maybe they eat junk food three meals a day. Maybe they neglect their homework and earn poor grades. You can love that person and yet still be careful to avoid letting them have a negative influence on you. Be a filter: pick and choose what you allow to influence you.

I grew up in a family with very complex and troubled parents, and I had to choose which lessons to take away from that experience. My dad didn't want me to end up as he did, so he forced me when I was eight years old to watch him shoot up heroin as a way to scare me away from it. When I was eleven, he took me to the Burnside bridge in downtown Portland—this is an area of town where a lot of homeless men and women live—and he said, "This is what you're going to become if you don't get educated." Of course, my dad wasn't walking his talk. As a drug addict, he wasn't capable of being a good role model. But he did what he could—in this case, by scaring the shit out of me! And it worked. I chose to learn the healthy lesson of avoiding drugs and excelling in school.

PAY ATTENTION! GOOD INFLUENCE IS ALL AROUND

Of course, it's easier to see the lessons inherent in extremely negative, dysfunctional situations. No one dreams of becoming a heroin addict. But it can be more difficult to spot the *good* influences when they show up. When something is going smoothly, or someone is treating you well, it can be easy to take it for granted. It takes some effort to open your eyes and really see these positive influences—but it's absolutely worth it. We need to see what is possible if we're going to get into the habit of shooting for the stars.

One of the most profoundly influential people in my life is my aunt Gail. Like me, she grew up within an alcoholic, abusive family, but she graduated high school and went on to college and a successful career in the military. When I was eight years old, Aunt Gail took me to visit the campus of San Diego State University in California. Even though I was so young, that was a life-altering experience for me. It was that very moment that I decided I would graduate from high school and go to college. From that day forward, I fell in love with school, because it gave me a hopeful vision for my future. I bet Aunt Gail had no idea that, just by sharing her college experience with me, she planted the first seed of success in my heart.

At about this same time, my uncle Rick took me on a retreat to a place called Prayer Rock in California. My uncle became a Christian after going down a self-destructive path, and he felt that God saved his life. Though I've never belonged to a particular religion, I've always believed in "something" and had an intrinsic belief in a higher power. At this retreat, my uncle and I talked about God, faith, and life. Not only did we have bonding conversations that were not typical for an eight-year-old and an adult, but he presented a bigger way of thinking, which was new to me. I'd been resistant to going to a church retreat, but this experience opened my heart to spirituality and helped me feel connected to something bigger than myself.

YOUNG ADULTS TALK ABOUT...THE MOST INFLUENTIAL PEOPLE IN THEIR LIVES

"Almost every human I interact with is an important influence in my life. You can learn and grow from every individual on earth. Everyone has a story that can shape yours for the better if you let them."

"Most people would say that their parents are the most important people in their life. But, for me, my relationship with my parents has never been positive. We've never looked at things from the same perspective, which causes a lot of tension. However, because I do live with them and their opinions are the ones I hear most often, I have let their perspective influence me. It was not until later that I realized it was in fact a negative influence that put me in a very unhealthy state of mind. Sometimes, even though those who are close to you are giving you their opinion out of endearment, it might not necessarily benefit you as a human being."

"My parents are important influences. Although they may not agree with my decisions sometimes, they can also be my best friends, cheer up my day, and provide me with support."

"The most important influences in my life are the friends I've met in recovery, Camille Adana, and my mother. All of these people inspire and influence me to make healthy decisions about my body and my life and to be the best person I can be. They provide me with amazing advice and support."

BE A FORWARD THINKER

Our lives are important at all points. Your teenage years and early twenties are meaningful times. But I want you to be forward thinking. You've got to think past high school, because these four years are just a sliver of reality. But at the same time, it's also one of the most influential times in your life. Enjoy it. Take what you can from it. But think to the future to avoid getting unnecessarily wrapped up in the present-day drama.

I recently met with a former student of mine who'd graduated eight years earlier. He said that if he could go back to high school, he wouldn't sweat the small stuff and the drama. Looking back from an adult perspective, he realized that he had wasted precious emotional energy on things that didn't matter in the end. Back then, he was in the closet about his sexuality. Instead of being true to himself, he wasted time living a double life and trying to force himself to date girls when he knew in his heart that he was gay. Despite the secret he was keeping, this student was a confident extrovert. He loved to dress fashionably, and he wasn't afraid to be a little "in your face." But he took a lot of crap for that from the less-confident students. That's because, if you're confident, that can trigger other people's insecurities, because they see what you have and compare themselves, and it's obvious to them that they don't measure up. That's okay. This student knew that it wasn't his problem. But still, he was alone. Even though he was fantastic, he didn't have anyone he could talk to about the real stuff.

Luckily, this student was a forward thinker. He didn't let the drama break him. In fact, he's even more himself—he's a fashion designer in New York City, and he's openly gay. He didn't repress who he was, and because he endured the social hardships of high school and didn't let the drama distract him, he's living his dreams.

LOOK AT THE INFLUENTIAL PEOPLE IN YOUR LIFE

When I was in high school, I knew I wanted a career as a teacher. So, what I did was make a list of all my teachers and write down all their positive attributes. Even those teachers who were perceived as mean or scary, or whose subjects I hated, I found their good qualities. I loved the teachers who got involved in extracurriculars, who were strict and had high expectations, who wandered around the classroom and showed attentiveness to the students. I loved teachers whose philosophies were authentic to them, who made their content relevant, and were unbiased in their approach to their subject. I ended up loving all of my coaches and teachers.

Now that I'm a teacher myself, I know more about what goes on behind the scenes. Your teachers, coaches, counselors, and so on— they're all people, living their own lives and experiencing their own hardships. They might be going through a divorce. They might be experiencing illness or financial difficulty. They may be trying to raise their own kids. They're affected by the news and politics and societal pressures, just like you are. But when they show up at school and walk through those doors, they try to set aside their personal lives as well as they can. I tell you this because it's important to keep perspective on the influential people in your life. Look at them from all angles. Take the good examples that they offer and leave the rest of it behind.

DO NOW! ANALYZE YOUR INFLUENCES

Make a list of the important people in your life: family, friends, teachers, coaches, bosses—anyone who has an influence on you. Now, go through the list and analyze each person, one by one. Be really honest with yourself. Is that person a positive role model? Do they bring out the best in you? Are they living their life in a healthy way? If the answer is "yes"—great! If the answer is "no," that's good information to have. It doesn't mean you need to kick that person out of your life. But it means you can be mindful to not let them influence you in a way that takes you off your life's path.

DO NOW! WRITE A GRATITUDE LETTER TO A POSITIVE INFLUENCE

Write a letter of gratitude to someone who has been a good influence on you. You can choose to send the letter or keep it to yourself.

To my students, teachers, and colleagues (past and present) at Cleveland High School in Portland, Oregon:

Cleveland High School is important to me for many reasons. Not only am I grateful that I'm currently a health and leadership teacher, but I'm very grateful to have been a student at Cleveland. Back in the 90s, this institution was a lifesaver. My parents were doing the best they could to take care of our family at home, but Cleveland did a fantastic job of taking care of me when I was there. My teachers, coaches, and teammates were my second family, and CHS supported every part of my identity—as a student, an athlete, and a person. It was such a wonderful experience, I set myself the goal of earning my Bachelor of Arts in health and physical education with a teaching certificate in secondary education. I knew in high school that I would return to CHS to give back to the place that had given so much to me.

I started teaching at Cleveland at age 21 and have loved every minute. I am actually in love with the school. The smell, the nostalgic feeling with every passing season, the chaos of Powell Boulevard, the teachers who represent our school, the coaches who constantly give 100 percent, the extracurriculars such as choir, band, and drama and how successful they are every school year. The administrative team that allows us teachers to teach and coaches to coach within our personality type and philosophy. How much our counseling staff gives to the student body outside of the academic rigor. The clubs and committees that allow students to find a way or an identity within our school. Jan Watt, who is on year 47 at Cleveland and is passionate about our school's success and respectability in our community. Then there are the wonderful parents who play a major role behind the scenes and make Cleveland a desirable school to attend. Cleveland is a dream, and I know it is, because it is truly a major part of my personal identity.

But what I love most about Cleveland are the students. I have the deepest love for them. Whether or not they are in my class, the students know that I have an open-door policy, and that I would do and give anything to help them—emotionally, mentally, athletically, academically, and socially. I care about their current realities and how they are going to use ADANA Dynamics in their lives. I inspire and motivate my students, and they do the same for me. It's a reciprocal relationship. There is a give and take between me and Cleveland students. We work together; and the conversations, bonding experiences, lunch meetings, and appointments are a work in progress to inspire one another. It touches my heart to see those students take that love out into the world.

My heart bursts with all of my love for Cleveland, the staff, the parents, the community, and most of all the students. Warriors, you are so important. I want you to be happy and I absolutely want the best for you.

Love,
Camille Adana

SEE THE GOOD IN PEOPLE

With over seven billion people in the world, chances are you're going to have to spend some time with people you'd rather avoid. Whether it's our parents, siblings, teachers, classmates, or coworkers—there are circumstances where we can't choose our company. We just have to make the best of it. One way to do this is to see the good in people. When we focus on a person's positive traits, we get into the habit of switching our perceptions and viewing the world in a more optimistic light—two crucial ingredients for happiness.

SEE THE INNER CHILD

If you're dealing with a hard situation with a person, it can help to picture him or her as a child. This can help cultivate compassion because it takes you back to a time when they were young and innocent. It's hard to be mad at a child.

I came from an abusive home, but that abuse didn't come out of nowhere. It was a repeated pattern that both of my parents brought into the relationship. When my mom and dad got together, they were both teenagers, living the hard-partying lifestyle of the 1970s. They were still practically kids themselves, and neither had healed from the trauma of their childhoods. My mom grew up in an environment of low expectations, poverty, and alcoholism, and was sexually abused by her stepfather. My dad had his own share of hardships: His parents both died young due to complications from alcoholism; he started using heroin when he was 17; and when he was 18, he found out that his dad wasn't his biological father.

When my mom was just 16, my dad swept her off her feet. He was 19 years old at the time, and she thought she'd found her prince charming. Reality set in, though, when my mom had me—a premature baby, weighing less than four pounds—and then my brother just eleven months after that. Suddenly, these two young people had the major responsibility of parenthood. To complicate matters, their partying lifestyle was gradually descending into a hell of serious drug and alcohol abuse, and neither had the familial stability or coping methods to handle life.

As much trouble as we had in our family, we had a lot of openness between us. My parents shared details about their own troubled upbringing that allowed me to walk in their shoes and see them first as children and then as teenage parents. It shifted my perception of them. I realized that they were both locked into painful pasts that they couldn't escape. They hadn't gone through the type of emotional processing and developing that I've done in my life, and which I've encouraged in my students, and now my readers.

When you're dealing with a hardship and conflict in a relationship, stop for a moment and think of that person as a child. I realize that my home life is an extreme example, but I share it with you to show that, no matter how low-functioning or troubled a person is, you can tap into your compassion and understanding of them. It's like entering their body and seeing life through their lens. That's where forgiveness begins.

DO NOW! WRITE AN "I SEE YOU" LETTER

Write a letter to a parent or guardian, telling them about some or all of the good things you see in them. Put it in a place where they'll be sure to find it. Surprise!

SEE THE GREATNESS UNDERNEATH

No doubt about it, my dad was a scary guy. Many times I watched him beat and almost kill my mother. I watched him jam a rifle down her throat. I watched him try to drown her in a sink. He forced me to watch him shoot up heroin, and I once witnessed him break a man's knee during a drug deal. I was terrified of him. As I can recall, I had only four meaningful moments with him where I felt really bonded. Other than that, our whole relationship was based on fear.

But he also, in his own way, taught me valuable life lessons. One day, our family was walking toward the bus, and along the way I made fun of a homeless person. My dad stopped me and said, "Don't you ever judge. That could be Jesus Christ testing you." After that, I didn't want to judge people. In part it was because I was so scared of my dad, I didn't want to disobey him. But looking back on it, I can see that he was right about this one. He pointed out that there is potential greatness under the surface of even the most humble human being. This is a good exercise in seeing the good in people.

FOCUS ON THE GOOD QUALITIES

Maybe you and your parents fight a lot. Maybe your siblings drive you crazy. Maybe you hate your teacher or your coach. Well, chances are, you're just looking at a small sliver of that person. They may have traits or behaviors that you can't stand, but you have the power to shift your perception and open your eyes to their good qualities.

Even though my mom contributed to our chaotic home life by abusing alcohol and instigating screaming matches with my dad, her many good qualities have always been apparent to me. She is the strongest woman I know, and she navigated a no-win situation the best she could. She stayed with my dad because he threatened to kill all of us, including himself, if we left, and so she did her very best to raise us despite the difficulties. She has always accepted me and encouraged me to be myself, no matter the stage of my life journey. I can talk to her about anything. She is one of the most amazing listeners I've ever known—so compassionate and nonjudgmental.

Because I was able to see my mother's good qualities, I could appreciate and love her despite all the hardship we were in. If you look around at the significant people in your life, I'm betting you can come up with a list of their positive qualities.

EXERCISE EMPATHY

It can be helpful to think about life from another person's perspective and try to see it through their eyes. One of the first activities I do with my students at the beginning of the year is to have a snowball fight with them. But these aren't your typical snowballs. What we do is, each student takes out a piece of paper. They don't write their name on it—this is an anonymous exercise. I ask them to write a list of what makes up their identity. This can be anything that is meaningful to the person—something they're passionate about, a hardship they've withstood, and so on. Once everyone is done, I have them crumple up the paper into a snowball, and then we have a snowball fight. After that, each person picks up a snowball, uncrumples it, and reads it to themselves. Then I ask them to read aloud two statements that stood out to them. It's incredible what comes up: *My mom killed herself. My sister cuts herself.* And so on. There are a lot of painful events that have greatly affected that person's sense of self. The point here is that, in revealing these deep, personal details, the students get a wider perspective on their classmates. They get to see their commonalities. They experience more empathy for others, as well as feel more compassion for themselves. They get to see that we all come to the table with pain and baggage. If we can keep that in mind and have empathy for every single person we engage with, then we can talk through our conflicts while maintaining a sense of compassion for all that the other person is going through as a human being.

HAVE COMPASSION—WITHOUT THROWING YOURSELF UNDER THE BUS

Of course, though I encourage you to see the good in all people, there are times when you have to make the tough choice to end a relationship. That can mean breaking up with a friend or sweetheart or even choosing to estrange yourself from an abusive family member. You can have compassion for all people, but that doesn't mean you should put yourself in harm's way. If you need to protect yourself by cutting ties with an unhealthy or dysfunctional person, you should absolutely do so. When you see life through that other person's lens, and you really feel you understand their struggles, it can be tempting to try to help them. While the impulse is noble, you have to practice discerning whether or not that person wants help. If they're not 100 percent committed to change, you might be pouring your emotional energy into a hopeless situation. Like I said, there are over seven billion people on this planet. You have to seek out those who lift you up, not drag you down.

DO NOW! SEE THE GOOD IN THE PEOPLE AROUND YOU

Think of a loved one with whom you have a challenging relationship. Take out your journal or grab a piece of paper, and write a list of all their best qualities. Keep your mind open and try not to forget anything. When you're finished, read through the list and really let it sink in. Tune into your feelings about this person and see if they've changed after taking the time to think about their greatness.

YOUNG ADULTS TALK ABOUT...SEEING THE GOOD IN PEOPLE

"Nobody is perfect. I often forget this and put my heroes on pedestals that crumble under the weight of reality. With time, I'm getting better at realizing people are just that—people! They're only human."

"I try to be open-minded and accepting of others or try to understand the place they are coming from. I try to refrain from judging people until I really understand their situation."

"My relationship with my parents is very strained and we fight, but what they do and say is important to me. They're the motivation I have to keep going to school and to graduate, because they didn't and I want to do better than that."

BELIEVE THAT EVERYTHING HAPPENS FOR A REASON

When you're going through something difficult, it can be hard to believe that it's happening for a reason. But once you walk through the experience, you can look back and connect the dots. There's a positive angle to every single circumstance—but sometimes it takes time to see it. In the present moment, you just have to act on faith that it's all adding up to something meaningful.

EMBRACE—DON'T RESIST

Life is dynamic. As we evolve, things change and eventually end. If you truly believe that everything happens for a reason, these transitions will be less painful. You'll embrace—not resist—the lessons and opportunities inherent in change. You'll be less likely to cling to something that isn't working if you see that loss as purposeful. If a romantic relationship or friendship comes to an end, you can choose to see that as the universe telling you that you need to focus your energy in a different direction. If a sweetheart cheats on you, that's a clear communication that he or she isn't the right partner. If a teacher or coach is critiquing you, you can choose to take that in as a lesson instead of feeling hurt or defensive. There's a message in everything, but you have to train yourself to hear it.

TAKE ADVANTAGE OF THE LAW OF ATTRACTION

Everything that's happening before our eyes is an external sign of what is happening in our inner world. This is what's called the "law of attraction," which is a philosophy that says "like attracts like." Or, in this case, "like *creates* like." Think about it—have you ever had a time where you went out into the world in a horrible mood, and then you had a conflict or argument with someone in an equally horrible mood? There's a feedback loop between your attitude and your experience of the world. So, if you change the attitude, you'll change the world you live in.

The universe is constantly communicating to us. For example, if your sweetheart breaks up with you, it may be the universe communicating with you. What message can you take from the event? Perhaps the universe is telling you that your sweetheart wasn't a good match for you, or that your family needs you right now, or that you should be prioritizing your academics. Or let's say you want to be valedictorian, but then you get a B in chemistry. Maybe that's the universe's way of communicating to you that, if you really want to reach your goal, you've got to step up.

After I started writing this book, I began dating a woman who was going through hardship and a major life transition. Her reality became my focal point, and that's okay because I'm a compassionate human being and I can do that. But the universe was probing at me, at my heart and my mind, telling me that I had to finish this book and accomplish my dream. I had diverted my focus away from the book because I was really invested in making things work with the woman I was dating. But then, I noticed she was distancing herself from me. She was preoccupied. She didn't have time for me. All the while, I was thinking, "I've GOT to finish this book. I want to make an impact on millions."

Then, all of a sudden, she ended the relationship due to personal circumstances. We broke up, and I had to move out of the home we shared together. I was devastated and heartbroken. But as time went on, I realized that the breakup was a signpost, pointing me in the direction of accomplishing my dream. I had a book to write, and perhaps this was the universe's way of telling me that I needed to focus on it. Perhaps my former sweetheart and I will reconnect in the future when the time is right. You never know.

There are beautiful, hidden messages in your universe. We have to believe that everything is working for us, not against us. It helps you get through hard times. Everything that comes your way is information from the universe; you can choose to feel good or bad about it.

TAP INTO YOUR PERSONAL BELIEF SYSTEM

Spirituality is an important component of personal development. This can be a religious tradition you were raised in (or one you adopted), but it can also include any spiritual practice that allows you to feel connected to a higher power. This can look different for people. Perhaps it means praying to God, meditating in quiet contemplation, connecting with your artistic muse, or getting in touch with nature. I've had my most spiritual moments at the beach at night, with a fire, looking out at the stars and moon. It makes you realize how small you are. Your problems loom large when it's just you, but when you have those moments when you zoom out and see yourself in context with the universe, it makes you realize that your problems are manageable.

WHEN YOUR BELIEF IS CHALLENGED...

Even if you truly believe that everything happens for a reason, there will be times when this philosophy is challenged. For me, this happens when a student dies, which is a too-frequent occurrence. A past student of mine, Alex Rovello, was an incredible tennis player and human being. He was a four-time state champion while at Cleveland High School and went on to play for University of Oregon. He was one of the top players in the country, with his whole life ahead of him, when he died cliff-diving. As hard as I try, I cannot see a reason for Alex's death. As far as I can tell, it seems like nothing more than a tragic loss.

I don't have answers here, just like his parents and community don't have answers. But what I *can* take from this experience is a lesson: it has taught me the importance of talking to teenagers about the realities of risk-taking. Alex took a calculated risk—he had researched the dive beforehand; alcohol played no role in the accident.

Alex's death made me realize that though teenagers can and should take risks in their lives, it's up to me as a health teacher to talk about it in a straight-up way. Teenage boys take bigger risks than girls and adults do because of their maturity levels, brain development, and testosterone levels. According to Dr. Frances E. Jensen, neuroscientist and author of *The Teenage Brain*, the human brain isn't fully mature until people are in their twenties. In an interview with National Public Radio, she said that the frontal lobe, which controls decision-making, is the last area to be developed. Signals move more slowly there. She says, "Teenagers are not as readily able to access their frontal lobe to say, 'Oh, I better not do this.'" Which is why, though they might be able to look back and realize the negative outcomes of a decision they made in the recent past, they might find it harder to make the right decision in the moment. And if they're high or drunk, that makes it especially hard to differentiate between a good or bad decision. But if they practice their decision-making regularly, there's a greater chance that they'll be able to call upon those skills even when their judgment is impaired by substances. I don't mince words with boys because I realize now that these kids aren't realizing the impact that ripples out in their lives when something major happens to them. If I can make that impact on a kid, then at least some good came from the loss of my student's life.

So, even when you can't see the reason for something, keep faith that the reason is there—it might just be invisible to you. The best you can do is take what you can from a hard situation.

YOUNG ADULTS TALK ABOUT...HOW SPIRITUALITY HELPS THEM THROUGH HARDSHIP

"I believe in the power of the universe. Energy is around us constantly. Find the positive energy in yourself and people around you, and your life will be forever changed for the better."

"Being spiritual helps me get out of my own head. I can seek advice and wisdom from others who believe similarly to me."

"My mother has always taught me that everything happens for a reason. This belief helps me bring better understanding to difficult times."

"I believe God puts us through hard times to make us stronger. If we couldn't deal with it, He wouldn't put us through it."

DO NOW! RELAX INTO THE PRESENT

No matter your personal belief system, you can practice meditation as a way to relax and tune into the present moment. Whatever hardship you're facing, it's easier to manage when you have a clear head and heart. You can do this quietly by yourself, or you can look online for guided meditations with an emphasis on breathing techniques and muscle relaxation. Focus on being still and on activating all five of your senses, Breathe deeply and fully, feeling your breath move through you. This has a calming effect on your body.

PART 2

DEAL WITH IT

Now that you've acknowledged your current reality, it's time to attack it and deal with it. We all know that life can be challenging, uncomfortable, sad, and frustrating at times. But the only way through hardship is to deal with it and face it head-on. This means taking 100 percent accountability for your life. I know this sounds tough and scary, but think about how *powerful* it is. You can't control all of the circumstances you face, but you have total power over how you respond. If you don't effectively process and deal with your emotions, they'll snowball and manifest in other ways—as health problems or as dysfunctions in your important relationships.

I know it might sound harsh, but when I tell you to "deal with it," I come from a place of love. I want to share with you some healthy strategies for getting through hardship by changing your mindset, enduring, finding positive coping methods, and getting inspired by fitness and motivational books. As you experiment with these strategies, keep in mind that what works for you is very personal. It's up to you to figure out how best to deal with what life throws at you. But I encourage you to take the healthiest approach possible and to really give yourself permission to cope with difficulties and move past them. Embrace this period of time, however long it takes, because it's a perfect opportunity to cleanse yourself and move forward. When you clean up your past, you clear the path for personal transformation.

SWITCH YOUR PERCEPTION OF A HARD REALITY

Letdowns are a part of life, and you've got to be able to process and get past your disappointments quickly. If you want to keep moving forward toward a better future, you can't get bogged down by past events and circumstances beyond your control. You've got to find a way to learn from every hardship and challenge you encounter. This is what I call "switching your perception."

EMBRACE—DON'T RESIST

When you embrace life, things flow. When you resist, that's when you bump up against conflict. As Eckhart Tolle says in his book *The Power of Now*, "Whatever the present moment contains, accept it as if you had chosen it." What this means is, instead of being angry or depressed about a circumstance beyond your control, act *as if* you had chosen that situation. For instance, let's say your sweetheart breaks up with you. Even though it's natural to feel heartbroken or rejected, you can challenge yourself to turn it around and switch your perception. This is a great opportunity to embrace the situation and get curious about it. *Okay, let's say I chose this breakup. Why would I have done that? Maybe it's because I want to focus on sports or schoolwork. Maybe it's because I want to spend more time with myself, or my family, or my friends. Maybe I knew deep down that he or she wasn't right for me, and I want to be single and available for the right person.* When you embrace what you face, you give yourself the opportunity to see the hidden benefits in an otherwise hard reality.

SEE EVERY ANGLE

When you face a hardship, it's easy to jump to conclusions and become entrenched in them. For instance, if someone breaks up with you, you might immediately think: "It's because I'm not good enough" or "They're a jerk." Instead of judging yourself and others, it's more helpful to think through all the angles. Do this with compassion and an open mind. You don't want to rationalize or excuse another person's bad behavior, but you do want to gain perspective so that you don't blame them—or yourself—unnecessarily. You can say, *Maybe they're going through a hard time right now. Maybe we have different interests or values. Maybe we have different communication styles.* You can hold up the experience and walk around it, viewing it from as many perspectives as you can imagine. When you switch your perspective, it's a lot easier to understand and believe that everything is going to be okay.

OPTIMISM IS EMPOWERING

Optimism is a key part of switching your perception. A positive outlook helps you feel good—or at least better—as you cope with a hard reality. But that doesn't mean you have to sugar-coat the situation or deny your feelings about it. Even when you've switched your perception, you may feel uncomfortable or scared or sad—that's okay. You've got to feel your feelings if you're going to process through them and let them go. But switching your perception is a deeply empowering action, because even if you can't control your circumstance, you can control your response. When you feel like you're in control, that's when you can make a thoughtful plan. When I face a hardcore circumstance in my life, I try to map out possible outcomes or think about why the universe is communicating with me in this way. Even though it's not comfortable, it eases my mind to know that I can control my perception and make meaning of the difficulty.

It's okay to find good in hardship. You might actually feel a rush of empowerment when you switch your perception of a hard reality. These rough situations, they have something to offer you, and you have the ability, imagination, and power to see and consider all the options and know that everything is going to be okay.

Most people wouldn't agree that a car accident is a good thing. When I got rear-ended, I thought, "That shouldn't have happened!" But then I went to a chiropractor and massage therapist, and I realized that the car accident had happened for a reason: I needed touch; I needed to be cared for in body and soul; and I needed healing. I wouldn't have known that if I hadn't had the accident. Over the course of six months of healing treatments, a lot of stuff came up for me. Emotions came up that I hadn't realized I was holding on to, and I sometimes found myself crying during those treatments, just letting go of those feelings. In the end, I was able to switch my perception of the car accident, because it had reminded me that it's crucial to pause and take time to care for yourself.

HOW DO YOU SWITCH YOUR PERCEPTION?

Switching your perception is simple, but that doesn't mean it's easy. When you're in a tough spot and you're flooded with feelings, it can seem almost impossible to put a positive spin on a situation or find meaning in it. You'll be tempted to stay entrenched in your negative feelings or cope in destructive ways that you'll regret later. I get it—it's hard. But I promise that, with practice, it becomes second nature to switch your perception.

When I want to change my perception, my first instinct is to write through it. Writing can be a cathartic release. Get out your journal and just go for it—blurt it all out. Get all those feelings out of your head and heart and down on paper. After that, take a deep breath and walk away. You can take a break from it for a day or two. When you come back and reread what you wrote, you can see how your feelings have evolved. Perhaps you'll relate to the situation differently once you've gotten past your initial reaction and had some time to process and reflect. Remember: embrace the reality, look at it from every angle, and filter it through an optimistic lens. Only then will you be able to switch your perception for the better.

ONE YOUNG ADULT TALKS ABOUT...
SWITCHING HIS PERCEPTION OF A HARD REALITY

"One important person in my life—or, at least, someone who *should* be an important person—is my dad. But my dad is not an important person in the way you'd think. You see, throughout my life, I've never had a role model, someone to lead me through life till I can be on my own. I've never had someone to tell me right from wrong, bad from good, the role of a 'man' and how to be one, or how to treat women. There was no role model present through my childhood and coming of age.

"But that's where the lesson is. You see, it's true what they say: actions speak louder than words. As I grew up, I learned that life is too short to wait for what you want. So I've spent the majority of my life trying to be something I've always wanted for myself: a role model. And this is very important to me because I'm trying not to repeat my family's cycle. I have six amazing sisters, all younger than I am. I think to myself, how do I want them to grow up and what kind of men do I want to see them with in the future? And without a doubt, I definitely want to be the kind of man that makes me smile when I think of him being with one of my sisters.

"So that's how my dad's actions have influenced me. It's been hard, starting from scratch and trying to be something. I believe that where you come from shapes who you are, and I am who I am today because of where I come from."

DO NOW! MAKE A PROS AND CONS CHART TO FACE A HARD REALITY

Think of a hard circumstance you're facing, or one that you faced in the past. Get out your journal or a piece of paper and make a T-chart of pros and cons of the situation. Examine it from every angle. Next, ask yourself: "What role did I play in this situation? What does this list reveal to me?" Take note of what comes up for you and how it makes you feel. This might be uncomfortable, but it's a good exercise for taking 100 percent responsibility for your life. If you contributed to the issue, brainstorm some ways that you can help repair it.

LET GO

In "Feel Your Feelings," we talked about connecting with and iden-tifying your feelings. Now we can talk about feeling *through* them and letting go. Though it's important to feel deeply and acknowledge what you're going through, you eventually have to decide where on the emotional spectrum to land. You can get locked into sadness and hopelessness, or you can take control of your thoughts and choose a better, happier mindset. I want you to feel your feelings. But don't hold on to them forever. It's important to find a balance so that a particular emotion doesn't overtake your life.

First, let's start with a "Do Now" exercise that will help you recon-nect with your feelings. Then we'll talk through some strategies for letting go of any feelings that aren't serving you.

DO NOW! OBSERVE YOUR FEELINGS

Find a place where you can sit quietly without interruption. Focus in on what you're feeling. Really tune in and get curious. Whatever comes up, don't judge yourself. Just step back and witness. Get deeper with it and ask why you feel that way.

HALT: ARE YOU HUNGRY, ANGRY, LONELY, OR TIRED?

If the feeling you observed was one you'd rather do without—maybe you're feeling sad or anxious or overwhelmed—it's time to check in and try to pinpoint the source of that feeling. "HALT" is a useful coping acronym for this. HALT stands for Hungry, Angry, Lonely, Tired.

When you're feeling down, you "halt" and ask yourself: Am I hungry? Angry? Lonely? Tired? If you're hungry or tired, your negative feelings can be heightened by your physical discomfort. If you're ruminating about something that angers you—especially if it's something that's not within your power to change—gently direct your mind elsewhere. If you're lonely, then it's time to reach out to a friend or loved one.

I recently got into a fight with my brother. It was late at night, just before I was heading to bed. I found myself unable to sleep because I was irritated and spinning out worst-case scenarios in my head. As you've probably already noticed, it's especially easy to feel bad at night when you're fatigued. Since I knew that, I was able to calm down by focusing on my breathing and telling myself that tomorrow would be a new day. I knew we could embark upon the experience with each other in a rested state of mind. And, of course, my brother and I worked through our problem the next day.

These kinds of calming techniques are imperative for relaxing yourself in the moment. You can circle back around to a challenging topic when your body and mind are in a rested, calm state.

REACH OUT AND CONNECT

Have you ever had an experience where you're feeling terrible about something, but when you share the problem with a friend, you realize it's not so bad? Sharing your feelings is a good way to let them go. Otherwise, if you stifle or repress them, your feelings will manifest in self-destructive ways.

Of course, it's important to be mindful of the person you're sharing with—make sure it's someone you trust and feel safe with. Tell them you've got something on your mind, and ask if they're willing to talk to you. Most likely, they'll be happy to help. Then, go for it—get it off your chest. You'll be amazed at the beauty that can arise in conversation. You might have an "aha" moment. Something within you might shift just from the power of speaking it aloud. You might realize that other people can relate to you. That person might give you valuable perspective that helps you see that you're blowing something out of proportion and need to humble yourself.

When you share your feelings with a friend, it does make you vulnerable. But vulnerability is the first step to intimacy. If you open up to a friend and he or she reveals themselves to be a compassionate, loving listener, then you've not only helped solve your problem, you've gained a new level of intimacy with someone. And then, when your friend needs the same kind of support, he or she will know that they can come to you. It's a beautiful, reciprocal relationship.

YOUNG ADULTS TALK ABOUT...LETTING GO OF HARD FEELINGS

"I often find that, without someone I trust to talk to, I will bottle up my emotions. But, when I have someone to talk to, like a therapist, I am relieved from the weight of everything."

"I find relief in surrounding myself with emotionally supportive people, and giving myself space and positive self talk. It's important to give yourself basic compassion."

"When I go through a breakup, my friends are supportive. They prove to me that I no longer need that person in my life and that I can be self-sustaining and independent."

"I try never to hold things in. Most of the time I have someone I feel comfortable talking to about what I am going through. Letting it out is very beneficial. It releases a weight of stress and helps me to process and deal with it."

DO NOW! MAKE TIME TO CONNECT

It's hard to find time in the day-to-day for an intimate conversation with friends, but it's something we all crave. You have to make a plan for it. Think of someone you want to bond with. Contact that friend right now and put out the invite. This can be a coffee date, sleepover, camping, beach trip—anything that will help you bond. Be sure to pin down an exact day and time, and really commit to following through.

DO NOW! WRITE A "THANK YOU" LETTER TO A SUPPORTER

Is there someone in your life who has been a rock for you during hard times? Write them a letter thanking them.

_____

Dear Josie and the Bocuzzi family,

Josie, you and I met my freshman year at Cleveland High School—first at volleyball practice and then during Spanish class. We clicked immediately. We were attached at the hip as best friends and teammates all through high school, and even went on to play college softball together.

I'll never forget the day you introduced me to your family—your mom, dad, and three older sisters: Anna, Apollonia, and Angie. The first time I went over to your house, Anna was singing opera to the cat at full-on, 100 percent volume. Apollonia came out of the bathroom with her shirt around her neck, her boobs hanging out, and two tampons in her nose. Mom was in the kitchen cooking one of her eight-course meals, wagging a dishtowel behind her like a tail because she was tooting. Everyone was speaking Italian. It was what I would come to expect as a typical day at the Bocuzzi house—loud, crazy, and bursting with amazing home-cooked food. It was awesome.

Bocuzzis, you took me in and made me a part of the family, and you showed your love by feeding me. Your home became my one solid source of food. When I was hungry, you took care of me. Josie, you and I used to have late basketball practices that started at five-thirty in the evening. So, when the ball rang at three o'clock, we'd go over to your place and eat a huge meal. I had solid nutrition because of your family. Not only that, but you've added so much joy to my life. I was always a serious little girl, and I never laughed so hard until I met you guys. You laugh so much! You live in the moment. You enjoy each other's company. You don't judge each other. You're truly my second family, and it's been so wonderful to be able to spend time with you and witness your family dynamics. Thank you for taking me in and making me one of your own. I love you and am forever grateful for the incredible influence you've had on my life.

Love,
Camille

LET GO OF EMOTIONS THAT DON'T SERVE YOU

Emotions are temporary. Think about a given day and how frequently your emotions, desires, and moods shift. That doesn't mean your feelings aren't important—they are. But there are times when you want to shake off a bad feeling. Maybe it's because you want to improve your mood. Maybe it's because you're feeling bad about a circumstance you can't change. Maybe you've been mulling over the same problem for weeks or months or years, and you're getting sick of it. These are all good reasons for just...letting go.

Of course, letting go is much easier said than done. But one technique you can try is a simple practice created by David R. Hawkins, a psychiatrist and spiritual teacher. In his book *Letting Go*, he recommends that you call to mind the unwanted emotion. Now, just sit with it—*without feeding the emotion with your thoughts*. This is the tricky part. If it's sadness you're feeling, connect to it, but do not think about the situation that makes you sad. When you feed the sadness with your thoughts, you can't let go of it. But if you sit the feeling and let it be, it'll naturally dissipate very quickly.

DO NOW! LET IT GO

Practice using Hawkins' technique for letting go. Find a comfortable place where you can sit privately. Call to mind whatever feeling you'd like to let go of. Hold the feeling in your awareness, but don't add to it with your thoughts. Take notice as the feeling begins to dissipate and float away.

DO NOW! CREATE A PHYSICAL SYMBOL OF YOUR PROBLEM...AND THEN DESTROY IT

Take a piece of paper and write down anything that's making you frustrated, irritated, sad, or angry. Now take the piece of paper and rip it up or toss it into a fire (of course, only do this with a fireplace *and* permission). Or, write it down on a piece of toilet paper and then flush it. Or write it on a soccer ball and then kick the crap out of that ball. (Of course, do all of this safely and use your common sense.) This can be something you do in private or as a bonding experience with friends or family.

ENDURE AND FIGHT THROUGH HARDSHIP

Hardship comes in many forms: heartbreak, illness, job loss, unrealized goals and wishes. It's an inescapable part of the human experience—and that's okay. This might sound unbelievable, but I'm actually pro-hardship, because it comes with so many useful lessons. It prepares you to be resilient in the face of troubles. It prepares you to work hard and stretch your limits if you're going to jump the hurdles that life sets up for you.

The more you can learn to get through hardship at a young age, the more practice you get in dealing with it during a time in your life when you have relatively easy access to resources for support. If you're in school and you're going through a hard time, you have a day-to-day schedule to keep your life structured; you're surrounded by counselors, teachers, and coaches whose job and vocation it is to give you the help you need. Plus, your brain is still developing during your teenage years, so you can still with relative ease shape your habits. (That's not to say you can't make positive changes when you're adult; it's just easier to lay a healthy foundation when you're young than to try to repair it when you're older.)

HARDSHIP IN FAMILY RELATIONSHIPS

Relationships are important and fulfilling, but they can also be a source of distress and hardship. This is especially true in the context of family, and even more so when you're young and dependent on your parents financially. If you're living in an unhealthy family dynamic like the one I grew up with, this can create real hardship in your life.

Of course, it's important to distinguish between an abusive dynamic versus more run-of-the-mill tensions that arise between loved ones. I'm sure you have no trouble thinking of at least one significant person in your life with whom you have conflict. The reality of relationships is that there are no two people who agree 100 percent about everything. We're all individuals with our own drives and desires. It's inevitable that conflicts will surface. Healthy confrontation is okay and natural— it doesn't feel good in the moment, but it may lead to resolution and increased closeness with you and your family. If you see something happening in your house, you can observe it—don't react. You can't control it. But you can witness and learn. Do the work to analyze the influence and decide which ones you want to repeat or break.

My best friend, Josie, is a very mellow person, but she grew up in a home where all conversations—whether they were arguments or not!— were conducted in loud voices. Her family has a lot of love, but they're not afraid to be confrontational. From a young age, Josie noted this as a dynamic that didn't suit her. She now has two kids of her own, and they're being raised in a very quiet household. This isn't to say that one approach is better than the other, but it is a good example of how we can choose whether to repeat or break the patterns we learned in childhood.

DO NOW! PROCESS YOUR FAMILY HARDSHIP IN A JOURNAL

Grab your journal or a piece of paper, and find a quiet place to contemplate. Write about a hardship that you've experienced (past or present) within your home life. What's the situation? Why is it happening? How can you make choices in your life (now or in the future) to do things differently or better? Take time to think critically about which cycles you want to repeat and which ones you want to break.

BEYOND ENDURANCE...

Back in 1997, when I was in my early twenties, I developed a chronic inflammatory skin condition called psoriasis. It causes dry, scaly patches that are red, painful, and itchy. Psoriasis is a hereditary condition, but it's also an emotional disease; it can be triggered or inflamed by stress or poor diet. And I was definitely stressed. My dad had recently died, my sweetheart had broken up with me, and my family had moved to Arkansas. When I developed this skin disease, it felt personal. Up until then, I'd spent my whole life hiding my problems and masking them by excelling in school and athletics. When I got psoriasis, I felt like it was tied to my personal identity. It was a physical manifestation of everything I'd tried to hide, as if my body were telling the whole world, "Hey, I'm fucked up."

This was the worst time in my life. It was awful enough that I seriously considered killing myself. But instead of giving into that defeatist mindset, I did my research. How was I going to overcome this? Then one day I happened to see an ad in the *Oregonian*, asking for test subjects for psoriasis research conducted by a local dermatologist. So I went. It was a very vulnerable experience that left me feeling exposed—literally—as researchers put me under ultraviolet lights, naked, and took photos of me. According to their metrics, I had 100 percent psoriasis. My entire body was covered with it.

In the truest sense of the word, my psoriasis was a dis-ease. I had so many stressors in my life, bottled up for so long, that they found an outlet for themselves. It was a symptom that I'd been in endurance mode for too long.

I share this story with you as a reminder that you can and must endure the hardships that you'll inevitably encounter. But life is more than survival. When you're in a bad situation, you must be proactive in finding solutions that will ease your pain. In my case, because I reached out to the dermatology researchers, I was fortunate to find a medical treatment that keeps the psoriasis in check. Just as this dis-ease forced me to take time for myself, you too must make time for self-care. Don't wait until your body rebels. Be mindful of your stress levels and your overall health, treat yourself with compassion, and take the time you need to heal from the hard situations you face. Otherwise, you burn out, because you're constantly in a state of "fight or flight." You can't spend your whole life with stress hormones coursing through your veins. If there is dis-ease in your life, you can endure in the moment, but put into place measures to better your life as soon as possible.

MAINTAIN FAITH THAT BETTER THINGS ARE POSSIBLE

No matter how hard your circumstances are, the worst thing you can be is hopeless. If you don't have faith that things can get better, it drains your motivation to change your life. The fact of it is, good comes around the corner. No matter how dire the present circumstance seems, there's an opportunity out there, just waiting for you to discover it. If I'd given up hope when I got psoriasis, if I had killed myself, I wouldn't have had the opportunity to become a teacher and coach, to become a role model, and to fall in love.

DO NOW! CREATE AN ENDURANCE CHALLENGE

Create a really big goal for yourself, something that will cause you to really stretch yourself. Hike twenty miles. Find a hill in your neighborhood and run up and down it, five to ten times, as fast as you can. If you force yourself to endure some hardship, you'll gain self-confidence by knowing that you can endure the challenges of life.

YOUNG ADULTS TALK ABOUT...THE HARDSHIPS THEY ENDURE

"I'm a recovering anorexic. Keeping myself healthy is a constant struggle. I have a good support system, and it's getting easier after each trigger to get back to a healthy place, but it is an uphill battle."

"Right now I'm facing being homeless. Again. It isn't easy for my family since my mom can't work and my dad is in another state and won't help."

"When I was six, a family member I was very close with died in a car crash. She was 66 years old and she took care of me three days a week. After she died, I had a really hard time coping with my feelings. I have a hard time connecting with my extended family because I don't allow myself to open up to them because I am afraid they will die."

"I have had multiple friends hurt my feelings and bully me. And the sad thing is, I don't know if they are even aware of how badly they hurt me."

"It is rare seeing my dad *not* drunk. He spends most of his time at the bar."

"Moving to America, my family expected change, but that never came. My mom drank every night and every day. She never came out of her room until she ran out of alcohol. One night, she and my older siblings were screaming at each other. I went downstairs and heard my brother yell, 'If you love me, you won't leave.' My mom stared at him silently, and then she turned and left. That was the night she wrecked her car and was in the hospital for three days."

"I have always had a wonderful family dynamic, which I am very grateful for. But because of a disability that an immediate family member has, I have had to mature faster than other kids and learn to be more independent."

BE PHYSICALLY ACTIVE

We start moving as soon as we come out into the world, and then we're crawling, walking, running, jumping, and climbing. Movement is integral to our existence as humans. Fitness is a feedback loop. If you can fall in love with movement, you can fall in love with life. When you're active, you not only improve your physical body—which improves your body image, energy level, and mood—but you gain the self-confidence that comes from knowing that you have the grit and determination to endure through physical challenges. Working out stimulates goal setting. Exercise—pushing yourself through physical activity—proves that you can endure, and you'll take that attitude out into your life.

I truly believe that every person can find some physical activity. Don't make excuses about it. There are accommodations for all people. Even if you have a profound disability, you can become empowered if you do find a physical activity. If you don't like to work out, that means it's time to do some detective work and find what works for you. Break a sweat and have some fun—whether that means joining a team sport, playing wall ball in the park, dancing in your bedroom, or hiking in nature. There's something for everyone.

THE POWER OF PLAY

There are two motives for fitness. There's fitness to play, and there's fitness as an endurance challenge. I always encourage people to fall in love with movement first—come to it as play—and then, if you desire, you can turn it into an endurance challenge.

I never knew what play was until my family moved next door to Brooklyn Park in southeast Portland when I was in sixth grade. Up until then, we'd moved around a lot, getting evicted from one place after another due to financial constraints and drug use. When we moved to our duplex in southeast Portland, I didn't know that it would be the first stable place that I would know. When I went to Brooklyn Park, I had no idea that it would have a huge impact on my life. I just adventured over there one day. The park takes up a city block, and has a baseball diamond, basketball court, jungle gym, and the "shack"—a small building filled to the brim with games, craft supplies, and sports equipment. It was here at Brooklyn Park that I first picked up a basketball. What started as play eventually grew to be my identity—I would go on to become a three-sport varsity athlete all through high school, and go on to college with an athletic scholarship.

I share my story to show you how serendipity operates in the world. Try out any and every mode of physical fitness that piques your interest. It doesn't matter if it's cheap and easy or fancy and expensive. If you want to geek out on gadgets, become a skier or cyclist. If you are muscular and are into weight-lifting, set that up on your own time and do it. If you want to revisit your childhood, break out your old jump rope or hula hoop. There's no right or wrong approach. The point here is to play and move your body. That's all there is to it.

ESCAPE INTO PHYSICAL ACTIVITY

As a teacher and coach, I've had an opportunity to witness the relationship between fitness and mood in the thousands of students I've had throughout the years. One of the trends I've seen is that the more sedentary a young person is, the more depressed, lethargic, and helpless they are. They make more excuses and have less confidence than the more physically active students. This leads to unhealthy coping methods.

Exercise is one of the best coping methods there is, in part because it increases endorphins—your brain's "feel good" chemicals. Endorphins suppress pain, heighten your mood, and strengthen your immune system. Our brains want us to be happy, and they help that process by producing these naturally occurring happiness drugs. I used to tell my dad, "I get heroin for free every time I work out. You should try it." If you exercise enough, you regularly supply your brain with these feel-good chemicals, which makes it easier to stay optimistic and happy.

When you're dealing with a problem, physical activity is one of the best ways to endure through hardship in a positive way. That's when you're pushing yourself, challenging yourself, coming to new places inside yourself. It can be a positive, healthy escape—unlike substances, which can be unhealthy escapes. Exercise is one of the only positive excuses to not focus on the bad—put your problems on the shelf temporarily and pick up your ball. Sometimes, when I was on the court back in high school, I was able to rip up my opponents because I was so pissed off at my home circumstance. I was taking a negative energy and transferring it into something positive. Of course, you don't need to follow my path, but find something that gives you that sense of release.

If you're into playing sports in a team setting or just with a friends, that's a way to be with other people without having to talk through emotions or process them. Sometimes you're sick of talking through your problems and you just want to get out, be in the sunshine with your friends, sweat, and have fun.

PERSONALIZE YOUR WORKOUT

Fitness is a lifelong process, and you can personalize your workout and mix it up as much as possible to keep things fresh and fun. Don't be afraid to explore and even risk making an idiot of yourself because you don't know what you're doing. Try a totally new fitness experience—if you're usually into yoga, give football a try, or vice versa. Try working out with and without music to get a different experience. If you usually work out solo, give team sports a try. Set yourself a challenge—if you're a runner, think about pushing yourself to do a marathon. As long as it gets your heart rate up and gets those endorphins flowing, it's fair game.

Of course, no matter which activity or sport you choose, it will require practice. Everyone who is great was once terrible. I know it doesn't feel good to be bad at something, but if you keep at it, you'll have a shifting experience. Pay attention to that shift. Don't forget it. And then, try to find a way to repeat it.

YOUNG ADULTS TALK ABOUT...THE ROLE OF PHYSICAL ACTIVITY IN THEIR LIVES

"My biggest treatment for stress is going out for a run or working out with music. It just relaxes me. Once I get home, I'm able to get my homework done."

"Running is very important for both my physical health and my mental body image. I just feel a lot better when I am working out consistently."

"When I'm sad or mad, I dance. I put all of my emotion and energy into the movement, letting my mind disconnect from my body and forgetting about everything."

DO NOW! GIVE IT 100 DAYS

No matter where you're starting out with your physical fitness, practice will help you improve. There's a fantastic website called Giveit100 (www.giveit100.com) where users create goals for themselves and then upload a daily video to showcase their practice and their progress. Whether or not you want to participate online, you can choose one aspect of your fitness, practice daily for 100 days, and take a video to record your progress. Or, if you're not interested in creating videos, you can use a journal to write down and track your progress.

DO NOW! PLAY!

Put down this book for a moment, and get up and play. Put on some music and dance. Do a few yoga poses. Shoot some hoops. When you get back to the book, your mind will be clear and you'll have gotten an endorphin rush that will get you pumped for achieving your goals.

READ MOTIVATIONAL BOOKS

My life changed the moment I stumbled across Jack Canfield's *Dare to Win* in a bookstore. I was twenty-one years old. I'd just developed psoriasis, I'd endured a long period of trauma, and I was feeling suicidal. I forced myself to get in my car and go to Barnes & Noble, where I went to the self-help section and found *Dare to Win*. It was as if I was being drawn there.

That book was a catalyst for me. It's all about no-nonsense goal-setting, and it's filled with stories of resilient people overcoming hardships. Reading it, I finally felt like I fit into this world. *Dare to Win* was my life in print, and it reinforced that I am okay, special, and unique, and that I'm an achiever who can continue to break cycles and go after my dreams. Talk about an influential book! I knew all the concepts—I'd lived them in my own life—but it was life-changing to see my experiences reflected on the page. I finally felt like I found the place where I fit in.

Motivational books can't do the work for you, but they provide inspiration and tools for you to do the work for yourself. I used the ideas in *Dare to Win* to change my own life. It reinforced my intention to be motivated from within and to do the work necessary for personal development. We create our experience of life through our thoughts, and when you supply your brain with inspiring, purposeful messages, it creates a positive impact on your decision-making, thought processes, and self-esteem. Finding, reading, and listening to motivational books (also known as self-help or personal development books) can improve any and every aspect of your life. If you have any confusion, weakness, passion, or curiosity, there's a book (or website, podcast, or video) that can help. In turn, you get to spend time exploring yourself, taking time for you, and improving your outlook on this beautiful, enduring life we live. Try it. Embrace it. You'll love it.

PERSONAL DEVELOPMENT IS A LIFELONG JOURNEY

Personal development is an ongoing process. Unfortunately, we're all so accustomed to instant gratification that, when a hardship occurs, it can feel like it's never going to pass. Allow it to feel terrible for a while. It won't last forever, but you have to give it its time. You have to let go of the concept of instant gratification and instead focus on the long game.

Your whole life is an education. There's a new challenge at every stage, and no matter the challenge, there's a personal development book to match it. Topics are incredibly diverse: how to improve self-esteem, manage your money, set goals and accomplish them, overcome weakness, process through grief, understand spirituality, cope with your past, lose weight, or improve you relationships or sex life. And that's just to name a few. Whatever your heart desires, whatever your stage of life, you can find it in a personal development book.

PERSONAL DEVELOPMENT TAKES PRACTICE

You can take some nugget of wisdom from every motivational book, article, or podcast that you encounter. Something about it will shift you and help you gain personal insights. The key, however, is active, focused engagement. This means creating a calm environment that's conducive to learning and self-reflection; an environment free from distractions and multi-tasking. It also requires deep engagement with the material itself. As you read or listen, try to absorb the concepts and stories that resonate with you. Finally, it's crucial to take the lessons and apply them to your life so you can be a more fulfilled person. You must do the work so you can embody the wisdom.

Lots of time, we know what we should do. We know how we want to feel. But it can be hard to get there. Personal development requires practice, just like most everything in life. For instance, for me, writing has always been a great practice for my personal development. I wrote through my feelings in a journal, and I wrote letters to the people in my life. By writing, I practiced processing and expressing emotion. It not only allowed me to help myself get through hard times, but it allowed me to get to know myself and to learn how to communicate effectively.

What about you? How best can you practice your personal development? That could be through writing, meditating, taking a walk in nature, processing your feelings with a friend—anything that allows you the time and space to contemplate and embody the lessons in the motivational books you read.

RECOMMENDED RESOURCES

There are an endless number of motivational resources out there, and I encourage you to be proactive and seek out the ones that resonate with you. Here are a few that I recommend:

The Aladdin Factor by Jack Canfield and Mark Victor Hansen
The Alchemist by Paulo Coelho
Anatomy of the Spirit: The Seven Stages of Power and Healing by Caroline Myss
The Art of Loving by Erich Fromm
Ask and It Is Given: Learning to Manifest Your Desires by Esther and Jerry Hicks
Awaken the Giant Within: How to take Immediate Control of Your Mental, Emotional, Physical and Financial Destiny by Tony Robbins
Born to Run: A Hidden Tribe, Superathletes, and the Greatest Race the World Has Never Seen by Christopher McDougall
Broken Open: How Difficult Times Can Help Us Grow by Elizabeth Lesser
Change Your Thoughts—Change Your Life: Living the Wisdom of the Tao by Wayne W. Dyer
Chicken Soup for the Soul by Jack Canfield and Mark Victor Hansen

Codependent No More: How to Stop Controlling Others and Start Caring for Yourself by Melody Beattie

Daring Greatly: How the Courage to Be Vulnerable Transforms the Way We Live, Love, Parent, and Lead by Brené Brown

Dare to Win by Jack Canfield and Mark Victor Hansen

Daring to Trust: Opening Ourselves to Real Love and Intimacy by David Richo

Developing the Leader Within You by John C. Maxwell

Don't Sweat the Small Stuff...and It's All Small Stuff by Richard Carlson

Eat, Pray, Love: One Woman's Search for Everything Across Italy, India and Indonesia by Elizabeth Gilbert

Embracing Uncertainty: Breakthrough Methods for Achieving Peace of Mind When Facing the Unknown by Susan Jeffers

Emotional Chaos to Clarity: Move from the Chaos of the Reactive Mind to the Clarity of the Responsive Mind by Phillip Moffitt

Expectation Hangover: Overcoming Disappointment in Work, Love, and Life by Christine Hassler

The Five Love Languages by Gary Chapman

Flow: The Psychology of Optimal Experience by Mihaly Csikszentmihalyi

The Four Agreements: A Practical Guide to Personal Freedom by Don Miguel Ruiz

The Happiness Advantage: The Seven Principles of Positive Psychology That Fuel Success and Performance at Work by Shawn Achor

Hardwiring Happiness: The New Brain Science of Contentment, Calm, and Confidence by Rick Hanson

Healing the Child Within: Discovery and Recovery for Adult Children of Dysfunctional Families by Charles Whitfield

How to be an Adult in Relationships: The Five Keys to Mindful Loving by David Richo

In the Meantime: Finding Yourself and the Love You Want by Iyanla Vanzant

Letting Go: The Pathway of Surrender by David R. Hawkins

Living, Loving, and Learning by Leo Buscaglia

Love: What Life Is All About by Leo Buscaglia

Loving What Is: Four Questions That Can Change Your Life by Byron Katie with Stephen Mitchell

A New Earth: Awakening to Your Life's Purpose by Eckhart Tolle

The Passion Test: The Effortless Path to Discovering Your Life Purpose by Janet Bray Attwood and Chris Attwood

The Power of Now: A Guide to Spiritual Enlightenment by Eckhart Tolle

The Power of Positive Thinking by Norman Vincent Peale

A Return to Love by Marianne Williamson

The Road Less Traveled: A New Psychology of Love, Traditional Values and Spiritual Growth by M. Scott Peck

The Seat of the Soul by Gary Zukav

The Secret by Rhonda Byrne

Self-Matters: Creating your Life from the Inside Out by Phillip C. McGraw

Secrets of a Millionaire Mind: Mastering the Inner Game of Wealth by T. Harv Ecker

The Seven Habits of Highly Effective People by Stephen R. Covey

The Seven Habits of Highly Effective Teens by Sean Covey

The Seven Spiritual Laws of Success: A Practical Guide to the Fulfillment of Your Dreams by Deepak Chopra

The Shadow Effect: Illuminating the Hidden Power of Your True Self by Deepak Chopra, Debbie Ford, and Marianne Williamson

The Six Pillars of Self-Esteem by Nathaniel Branden

Start Where You Are: A Guide to Compassionate Living by Pema Chödrön

The Success Principles: How to Get from Where You Are to Where You Want to Be by Jack Canfield

Success Is an Inside Job: The Secrets to Getting Anything You Want by Lee Milteer

The Three "Only" Things: Tapping the Power of Dreams, Coincidence and Imagination by Robert Moss

Think and Grow Rich by Napoleon Hill

Tuesdays with Morrie by Mitch Albom

Unlimited Power: The New Science of Personal Achievement by Tony Robbins

What I Know for Sure by Oprah Winfrey

When Bad Things Happen to Good People by Harold S. Kushner

When Things Fall Apart: Heart Advice for Difficult Times by Pema Chödrön

Wherever You Go, There You Are: Mindfulness Meditation in Everyday Life by Jon Kabat-Zinn

Wishes Fulfilled: Mastering the Art of Manifesting by Wayne W. Dyer

Some other great resources for inspiration are Oprah Winfrey's *Super Soul Sunday* and Mastin Kipp's "Daily Love" email (www.thedailylove.com).

DO NOW! BROWSE THE SELF-HELP SECTION

What issue are you experiencing in your life right now that could benefit from reading a self-help book. Take a trip to your local library or bookstore, or sit down for an internet search. Browse for a self-help book that speaks to your current need. Of course, once you get the book, the next step is to actually read it—otherwise it becomes an unhelpful piece of "shelf help."

TAKE A BREAK FROM TECHNOLOGY

Most of you reading this book are digital natives. Meaning, you've grown up using computers, the internet, hand-held gadgets, video games, and smartphones. It's probably hard to envision a life without constant access to these technologies. And since you've never lived without them, you may not be able to see their negative effects.

Over the years that I've been teaching, I've been able to witness the many ways that teenagers have been affected by the explosion in technology. The biggest problem I've seen is that they aren't talking face-to-face anymore. So much of their interactions take place online, and the biggest topic of offline conversation is what's going on on social media. This problem is compounded by the fact that much of what we see on social media is just a persona—you're not seeing the real person; you're seeing the face they've carefully constructed to show the world. As a result, friendships and communications are shallower and dramas are magnified. It can leave us all feeling isolated and disconnected.

Whether or not you're conscious of it, you're feeling the ill effects of our society's overuse of technology. As humans, we have an inborn need to be connected to the present moment and to have meaningful personal relationships. We crave it. And one way to reconnect with those needs is to take a break from technology. When you disconnect from the internet, you can plug into yourself. Without the constant flood of information coming at you, you can tune into your own inner quietude and do the deep work of personal development. Only when your mind is quiet will you be able to figure out what you value. How do you want to be treated and treat others? How do you want to give back to society? What are you passionate about?

FIVE SIDE EFFECTS OF TOO MUCH TECHNOLOGY

1. Overemphasis on Fun and Friendships: Technology is a distraction. You can't hone in and deal with your problems if you're constantly connected or distracted. If you're constantly on your phone, you're overemphasizing fun and friendships. This creates a skewed perspective on what is important and what you should truly be focusing on.

2. Lack of depth: Online friendships can be shallow and superficial. You need to bond in person. Think about all the videos you've watched and the articles and the status updates you've read. Was any of it important? Do you remember any of it? There can be a drop in self-esteem and quality of life if you're not connected to people in a deep and real way.

3. Delays in dealing with it: If you really want to deal with your issues, you've got to get real about how technology is distracting you from what's important. When you give into instant gratification, you delay dealing with your long-term challenges.

4. Lack of embodied presence: You can't settle down and be embodied in the moment if you're constantly swimming in the information stream.

5. Trolling: The internet has given rise to a total disconnect between real life presence and internet presence. Kids and young adults say awful stuff online that they wouldn't have the nerve to say in real life, and this breaks down self-esteem and friendships.

TALK TO YOUR PARENT(S) OR GUARDIAN(S) ABOUT TAKING A BREAK FROM TECHNOLOGY

When I tell my students to turn off their phones, a common response is, "My parents will be mad if they can't get ahold of me." It's true that, these days, parents and guardians expect to have 24/7 access to their kids, and they might worry if they can't reach you. So, think ahead. Don't just turn off your ringer. Instead, talk to them. Tell them you need some relief from technology. Not only is this a good opportunity to state your needs—which is always a good practice to have—but, more than likely, your parents will understand. They might be experiencing digital overload themselves. There's always room for creative problem-solving. Make a plan. Maybe your family chooses one evening a week where everyone agrees to stay home and off the computer, internet, phone, and so on. Or, if you plan to have a tech-free date at a friend's house, you can make sure your family can reach your friend's parents in case of an emergency. That way, you and your family can help each other honor your need to take a break from technology.

DO NOW! TALLY YOUR GADGET USE

Tally how many times you touch a gadget in a day. This is a good exercise in becoming aware of just how connected you are. Then, challenge yourself to trim that number—see if you can cut it in half. Notice whether you feel more present in your body the less you're engaged with your phone or other gadget.

DO NOW! HAVE A GADGET-FREE TABLE TALK

Technology lets you escape. In-person conversations allow you to truly connect—and that's a deep, human craving that we all have. Invite a few friends over. Collect their digital devices and put them in a box in a closet. Now, just hang out and enjoy each other's company for a technology-free couple of hours. Notice whether you feel a different sense of closeness with them. (And remember: If your parents or guardians might worry about not being able to reach you, make a plan for that. For instance, you can agree to check your phone at a particular time.)

DO NOT USE DRUGS AND ALCOHOL TO COPE

"Just say no." You've heard it so often that it's become a cliché. And yet teenagers and young adults are still using drugs. They're still curious. They're still experimenting. Instead of saying "just say no," I think it's time to have a more nuanced conversation. Let's get real about the role that drugs and alcohol are playing in your life.

HEALTHY SUBSTANCE USE

I'm about to say something controversial: I believe that you *can* use some drugs and alcohol in moderation. Shocking, I know, to hear that from a health teacher and fitness enthusiast. Of course, there's no good reason to ever experiment with hard drugs. There's no such thing as recreational use of methamphetamines or heroin. But, when you're an adult, you can enjoy a glass of wine with dinner or drink a beer or two with friends. No problem. As marijuana becomes legalized across the United States, it'll undoubtedly be more common to see the average person light up and have a few puffs to unwind.

So, I don't take a "just say no" stance. I take a "just say...later and in moderation" stance. As I've witnessed over the years, teens are more willing to push boundaries and explore substances in the extreme. They're more likely to binge drink. They're more susceptible to influence from their peers. They're *less* likely to think through the possible repercussions—getting in trouble with parents or the law; hurting or killing themselves or others. I've gone to many funerals for kids who've been killed because of recklessness. Teens and substances are a dangerous mix.

ARE YOU HAVING FUN, OR ARE YOU COPING WITH PROBLEMS?

You may think that you're drinking or using drugs because it's fun. You're partying with friends. You're having a good time. But I bet if you dig deeper, you'll see that you're using substances because you're coping with something. Some young people use substances because they feel awkward in social situations and need the "social lubricant" that alcohol and drugs seem to provide. Some use substances to cope with their fears about their identity, sexuality, academics, or the future. Others are escaping from hardship at home. It can seem like an easy answer to get wasted and get away from it all for a few hours.

One of the problems with drugs and alcohol is that they're *designed* to be a vehicle for escape. You feel great when you're high or wasted because that's what they were designed to do. It's not a special experience. It's not meaningful. It doesn't mean your life is substantially better. It's just a chemical reaction. You might feel good in the moment, but the risks are too great; they're not worth it. The more you choose drugs and alcohol, the more your brain becomes habituated to that choice, which leads to dependency and addiction. According to Dr. Frances E. Jensen, author of *The Teenage Brain*, "the effects of substances are more permanent on the teen brain." She says that "binge drinking can actually kill brain cells in the adolescent brain where it does not to the same extent in the adult brain." And, teenagers who use marijuana daily or frequently for a year or longer have decreased verbal IQ.

And...those problems that you were trying to escape from in the first place? They're still there when you wake up—only now they're compounded by a hangover.

What I want you to do is really think about it: Why are you drinking? Why are you smoking pot or using hard drugs? Dig deep and reflect on your reasons. You might come up with some painful answers. *I'm lonely. I'm scared. I'm unhappy.* Well, okay. It's not fun to uncover those painful emotions, but once you do, you can start to cultivate healthy coping habits that will serve you better and let you change your life instead of just changing your emotional state in the moment.

TALK IT OUT: PEER INFLUENCE IN ACTION

In my classroom, I do an exercise where I break out the students into three groups based on their drug and alcohol use. One group for non-users, one for medium or heavy users, and one group for those in the middle—the kids who partake every once in a while, or whose parents let them have a drink with dinner.

Then the discussion begins. Each group has an opportunity to express why they make their choices around drugs and alcohol. It can be awkward at first. The non-users are shy about speaking up because they think they're going to be seen as judgmental. The users are frequently defensive because they presume they're going to be attacked for their choices. But when both sides get talking, things get interesting. Whether they use drugs and alcohol or not, most kids find that, when they really explore their motivations, they have compelling reasons for their choices. This is where it gets juicy. Usually, no matter which side they're on, their choices are influenced by family dynamics. The kids who don't use, it's often because someone in their family has an addiction, or has gone to jail, or has died. They've seen how powerful the negative effects of substance use can be, so they opt out.

The part that makes me sad, though, is when the substance users are asked why they *do* use, their answers are telling—there's drug or alcohol use in their family; their parents know they're using and they don't stop them. Some parents even provide the substances for their kids. From my perspective as someone who's had thousands of students cross her path over the years, I've gotten to a point where I can tell instantly which ones will repeat their parental cycles. I see where they're at academically, who they hang out with, their self-esteem. Even at this young age, where teenagers feel like their whole life is ahead of them, I can see that they've started down a particular path.

STAYING ABOVE THE INFLUENCE

There's a hard truth here that deserves acknowledgment: When you're above the influence, you may not fit in right now. When your friends are getting wasted and it looks like they're having fun doing it, it's easy to feel left out. Even though you're making a good decision for yourself, it can feel like a punishment instead. This is a temporary state, though. When you choose positive coping strategies, you prove to yourself that you value your future health and happiness over your present-day desire to escape a temporary hardship. You'll benefit greatly in the long run.

DO NOW! IDENTIFY HEALTHY COPING STRATEGIES

A healthy coping strategy can be anything that helps you alleviate hard feelings without causing harm to yourself. Your healthy coping strategies are going to be unique to you, so you'll have to spend some quality time with yourself to identify the methods that speak to you. Maybe you cope by putting on some music and dancing your ass off. Maybe you go for a run to get that endorphin high. Maybe you feel best when you reach out to a friend or counselor for a supportive conversation. Maybe you feel best when you gather your thoughts through prayer, meditation, or by writing in your journal. When you know what works for you, you know where to turn when life gets hard.

YOUNG ADULTS TALK ABOUT...HEALTHY COPING STRATEGIES

"My self-care strategy is to do whatever feels good in the moment, whether that be a hot bath or a trip to the gym—whatever I need, I provide it for myself."

"When I was very young, I wanted to be my uncle. He was vibrant and could make just about anyone fall on the floor laughing. One day he asked me to promise him I would never involve myself in drug activity. I did just that, and to this day I plan on keeping that promise."

"I often dance or do something creative to relieve stress. Allowing my brain to unhinge and explore is an easy release for me. I also find great peace in nature. Getting out into the woods and breathing in fresh air is like a reset button for me. Everything starts working better."

"My number one self-care strategy is to stop and take a moment to check in with myself and make sure that I'm happy. If I'm not, I reassess the situation and see what I can do to make myself happy. Sometimes that's listening to music or watching a movie or going on a run."

DO NOW! WRITE A LETTER FROM YOUR FUTURE SELF

Envisioning your future can help you make better choices in the present. Imagine that you're ten years older than you are now. Write a letter from the perspective of your future self. In the letter, paint a picture of what your life looks like in the future, and share with your "past" self how the choices you made in your teens and early twenties affected your "future" self.

PART 3

ASPIRE

So far, we've talked through a lot of hard stuff. Acknowledging your current reality can dredge up difficult feelings. Dealing with it forces you to come face-to-face with your challenge areas. Take a moment to check in with yourself. What kinds of mindset shifts have you experienced so far? Take a moment to pause and think. Pull out your journal and take a minute to gather your thoughts. And be sure to give yourself credit for coming this far.

Now it's time to aspire.

This is where we can have some fun. When you aspire, you expand your sense of possibility and dream big in all domains of life. Maybe that means the career of your dreams, the sweetheart of your dreams, the family of your dreams. Maybe that means spiritual fulfillment, or travel and adventure. Anything! When you can envision your ideal life—and you truly believe that you deserve to reach that—that's when you'll feel the fire in your heart. Of course, you must take the practical steps to see your dreams through to fulfillment, but it all starts with aspiring.

PRIORITIZE YOUR LIFE

Life is a balancing act. No matter your stage of life, there's a lot of competition for your attention. That's why it's critical to identify what you value most and then set good boundaries so you can focus your attention there.

IDENTIFYING YOUR PERSONAL COMMITMENTS

Personal commitments are different for each of us. They're part of our unique makeup. What aspects of life are most meaningful to you? What are your burning desires and biggest dreams? Who are the most important people in your life? When you answer these questions, that's when you'll know what your commitments are. If you don't know what they are, you can't be certain that you're carving out the time and energy needed to tend to them.

Back in high school, I wrote down my list of top priorities. They went: (1) academics (2) athletics (3) family (4) friends and (5) sweethearts. This felt right to me. Your list might look completely different. But for me, I knew that academic and athletic success were my tickets out of the negative cycles of my home life. I love my family with all of my heart, but because there was so much dysfunction there, I couldn't put them first. It would have drained me. There was too much of a risk that I would repeat their cycles if they became my focal point. Similarly, if a sweetheart was a distraction to my academics or athletics, I knew I needed to put that relationship in its proper place.

You have to come up with your own personal commitments. You have to be a detective in your own life and figure out what *you* value. Your family and friends might have a different idea of what is important. That's okay. You can listen to the important people in your life and acknowledge their values, but you're not obligated to take them on as your own. You have to stand strong and respect yourself as an individual. Back in high school, my dad would have told me that family should be my number one commitment. Each of my coaches wanted me to be most passionate about their sport. But I had to choose to commit myself to the priorities that felt right in my heart—and you do too.

Be aware that some people might try to sabotage your personal commitments, whether or not they intend to. Other people have their own agendas and their own sense of what's valuable, and they might feel like they know what's best for you. When you make the time to list out your commitments, you can more easily figure out which situations and people are serving them—or undermining them. Seek out friends, mentors, and role models who you can trust to help you maintain your commitments without imposing their own values on you.

DO NOW! THINK OF A TIME WHEN YOU WERE MOST HAPPY

Find a quiet place to sit, free from distractions. Think of a time when you were most happy. Get really detailed about the scene. When was it? Who was there? What were you doing? What did you love so much about that moment? How does it exemplify something that you really value? For instance, perhaps one of your happiest times was a hiking trip with a friend. What does that say about you? Perhaps it's that you value nature, quiet time, good friends, and physical activity. Great. If you know those are your values, you can make a personal commitment to making sure those aspects are always present in your life.

SETTING GOOD BOUNDARIES TO SUPPORT YOUR PERSONAL COMMITMENTS

Once you've identified your personal commitments, you must put into place some good boundaries to help prevent them from being trampled on. When you prioritize your life according to what feels right for you, there will be people who don't understand, or diminish, or are even offended by your choices. They may try to drag you off-course with distractions, temptations, or put-downs. Perhaps you decide that academics are your top priority, and it causes friction with your friends because they want you to come out and party even though you know you need to stay home and study. That's okay. It can be frustrating or hurtful in the moment, but you have to remember that other people's reactions are their own. They're rooted in the other person's issues and have really nothing to do with you. You're the one who has to face the consequences if you let yourself down. Plus, when you set goals and priorities and assert the boundaries necessary for achieving them, it quickly reveals who in your life are high-quality, supportive people. Those are the ones who want you to reach your full potential.

DO NOW! MAKE A LIST OF PERSONAL COMMITMENTS

Make two lists. First, list out your ideal top commitments—meaning, those people and activities that should receive the most attention because they serve your best self and your biggest dreams. Next, list out your actual commitments—meaning, what are you actually prioritizing in your day-to-day life, based on how much time and energy you spend there. Compare the two lists and look for spots where they're out of sync. What changes can you make so that your daily life reflects your ideal commitments?

DO NOW! CHART THE 24 HOURS OF YOUR DAY

We have twenty-four hours in a day. How are you spending yours? Take out your journal or a piece of paper, and break down how you spend your hours. (This is an exercise I first encountered in Jack Canfield's *Dare to Win*.) First, consider how much time you spend doing the things you have to do—sleeping, going to school, participating in your extracurriculars, eating, doing homework, and so on. Add it all up. Now, do the math: how much time is left over? What are you doing in that time? Be honest with yourself and assess which of those activities are unhealthy or not a particularly great use of your time. What could be replaced with activities that are based in your personal development—physical fitness, academics, social skills, and so on?

YOUNG ADULTS TALK ABOUT...FOCUSING ON PRIORITIES

"I want to be a Division I baseball pitcher. So I don't drink, I don't smoke, I don't go to parties—because I have baseball. I just don't even go there."

"I want to accomplish so much, so I have to prioritize and take care of myself."

"I have to prioritize my health and not put too much pressure on myself. I'm a perfectionist, and I also have a mental illness—those things don't mix well together when I'm not maintaining a healthy mind and body."

SET SMALL AND BIG GOALS

When I first read Jack Canfield's book *Dare to Win*, I realized I was in the goal-setting club, which is only 2 to 3 percent of people. That's right—only a small minority of people actually have the fire in their heart and really strive to set and achieve goals. What I find interesting about my life, though, is that even though I'm in the 3 percent, because I grew up in a 97 percent family, I consider myself a 100 percent person. I'm a natural goal-setter, but I also understand the perspective of those who aren't naturally motivated from within. However, from my years as a teacher, I can tell you a lesson I've learned after observing thousands of students: If you're not a goal setter, you're living in the past and bitching about the moment. I know it sounds harsh, but it's true. Generally, people feel happiest when they're moving forward, when they've got momentum in their life. And nothing creates momentum like a goal.

If you don't have the motivation to be successful, I'm not sure what to tell you. I'm not sure anyone can help you. We can only control ourselves, so I have to be mindful that if you don't want my help, I can't help you. That's me, walking my talk. But if you've got even the smallest seed of ambition in your heart, I hope you'll tend to it and let it grow.

START BY CULTIVATING CURIOSITY

Some people have a natural passion in life. Others need to do some soul-searching. It's okay, especially when you're young, to not know exactly what goals you want to set and achieve. If you're intimidated by goal-setting, I ask that you do this: cultivate curiosity and pay attention to what zings for you. It's as simple as that. You don't need to do anything special. Just go about your life—but do so with a heightened awareness. Be an investigator. Pay close attention to the people, places, and things that make up your world, and see which ones excite you the most. Take opportunities as they arise. If someone invites you to try an activity you've never tried, give it a whirl. If you walk past a bookstore or library, pop in and browse a subject matter you know nothing about. You never know when you're going to stumble on your passion, but you can make the effort to create serendipity for yourself.

DON'T BE AFRAID TO SET GOALS

Throughout my time as a teacher, I've met a lot of students who are freaked out by the whole process of goal-setting. If you're not naturally inclined toward goal-setting, you might be tempted to just throw up your hands and say, "I don't know what I want, and I don't care."

My younger sister, Pearl, was a lost soul in high school. In many ways, she was like the majority of students who cross my path as a teacher. Pearl is an incredible human being, but she's always been a "live in the moment" kind of person. When she was a teenager, she hadn't yet cultivated the skill of forward thinking, and she wasn't able to articulate what she wanted to accomplish in her four years of school—or in her life after that. Pearl was a good student in elementary and middle school, but in high school, all she cared about was her social life. She's an extroverted social butterfly, and the relationships in her life took top priority. Of course, relationships are important to all of us—and they should be—but with Pearl, as with so many people, her commitments were out of balance. She didn't put any emphasis on academics, career, or financial goals. And so, even though she's intelligent, she got straight Fs on her report card and didn't graduate from high school.

Pearl's situation was compounded by the death of our father when she was only sixteen. They had an incredibly close bond, and she was, of course, devastated when he overdosed on heroin after not using it for thirteen years. This hardship paralyzed her growth as a student, and she gave up on herself.

Now in her thirties, Pearl is a wonderful mother to two children. She has one domain of life figured out—family. But she's not fulfilled with the other domains. She doesn't have a career or financial independence. And because her life lacks balance, she's not as happy overall as she'd like to be. If she'd done the hard work of practicing her goal-setting in her younger years, she'd be in a better place in life right now. Pearl just got her GED in her early thirties, and it was hard for her to carve out the time, energy, and focus from her busy adult life to go back and revisit that learning that she could and should have done decades earlier.

In some ways, Pearl is a cautionary tale for how a fantastic person can sabotage themselves by neglecting to think about their future. She's really the epitome of the students I see, who say, "I don't really care about tomorrow. Whatever." Being in the moment is a great quality, but it also has a negative side. If you don't temper your present-focus with some longer-term thinking, you can't achieve your goals and feel fulfilled across all Six Fs: Future, Fitness, Friendships, Family, Finances, and Fun.

Some people find their passion early. Others, like my sister, don't. If you're lost at a young age, you have to do the work at a young age. High school and college are the times when you have the most access to support—teachers, academic advisers, counselors, and coaches, all on hand to help YOU succeed. Take advantage of it. Because, if you get out into the adult world and haven't figured out how to set goals and go after them, you likely won't recover.

YOUNG ADULTS TALK ABOUT...THEIR BIGGEST GOALS IN LIFE

"My goal is to go into psychology and do research and work with trauma, anxiety, and eating disorders.

I will for sure one day go to Democratic Republic of Congo and work with those affected by war."

"I want to be the first girl in my family to graduate high

school and go to college. I want to make something out of myself and make my loved ones proud."

"My goal on a personal level is to strive for a healthy, stable mental state and be surrounded by positive people who can influence me to be better. However, on a larger scale, I want to be able to influence others with my experiences. I want to help them realize the importance of the things they are going through and to know that life is a roller coaster and your body and mind come first before anything else."

"I am hands down a goal setter. I set goals every time I step out of bed in the morning. I have so many, it's quite challenging to highlight just one. I guess a main goal of mine, which people overlook at times, is to simply be happy. When one feels complete and utter happiness, they are unstoppable. That bliss helps one follow their dreams in other aspects, so I couldn't wish to have anything better than complete happiness for myself and others."

"My goal in life is to be able to live a life of freedom, one where I have the financial means and career opportunities to allow me to travel and explore."

"I want to get married and have the most amazing and connected relationship, one that is very healthy, where we are individuals but also one. And kids. Lots of kids."

CHECK IN ON YOUR GOALS ON A REGULAR BASIS

It's not enough to set a goal. That's just the first step. After that, you've got to regularly check in with yourself, your mentors, and your accountability partners to make sure you're on track to achieve those goals. When I was a high school athlete, two of my coaches—Linda McLellan and Katie Meyer—held goal-setting meetings pre-, mid-, and post-season. Every player wrote down their goals around skill-building in that sport, and then we talked about them with the coaches. This was an incredibly valuable experience. Those conversations helped cultivate intrinsic motivation in the players, because we were setting goals for ourselves. They weren't being imposed on us by any outside force. Plus, it helped us stay future-focused and not get stuck on past mistakes and letdowns. We were first and second team All-City/State every season, every year. This goal-setting and accountability helped me be the MVP of the league in volleyball and in softball my senior year, and first and second team all-state every year.

GOAL-SETTING IN ALL SIX DOMAINS OF LIFE

When you're in high school, there's a big emphasis on education as the path to a career. However, it's important to set goals for all of the Six Fs (Future, Fitness, Friendships, Family, Finances, and Fun). You are a whole person, and it's important to tend to all of these domains in order to live a balanced life.

Once you've identified your goals, you have to figure out the step-by-step process. This depends on what a person is trying to accomplish. For example, I frequently hear my students say they want to get married. They look forward to that. Or, they want to travel the world after high school. These are two fantastic goals. But the question I ask is "how"? How are you going to get that rock? How are you going to figure out if this person connects with you? How are you going to finance your trip around the world? I don't ask "how" to dissuade people; I ask them to actually have them answer the question, because, if you can answer the question, you can actually do it. Some people's behavior and decision-making is completely contradictory to their dreams. If you sincerely want to fulfill a goal, you have to spend some time figuring out the "how."

That's where helpers come in. Once you know what you want, you can pinpoint the right person who can help you achieve it. If it's an academic goal, reach out to a teacher. If it's a fitness goal, reach out to a coach or a person in your life who is a good model of fitness. If it's an emotional goal, reach out to a counselor or a supportive family member. These are the types of people who can help you break a big goal into its smaller, more manageable components. You might be pleasantly surprised when you realize just how much these people in your life want you to be successful—and are willing to do anything they can to help.

Even though, as I mentioned earlier, I'd had a shifting experience when I was eight years old and visited San Diego State University with my aunt—which formed in my mind the goal to go to college—it was really through the help of incredible role models and mentors that I actually got to college. One of my teachers, Jan Watt, made it her mission to get me into college. I knew I wanted to go, but I had no idea how to get there. Jan helped me get my college recommendations; she taught me what financial aid was all about; she helped me pay for the college applications if there was a fee; she helped me apply for scholarships. And with Jan's help, I won six different scholarships, and I ended up at Concordia University on a full-ride academic/athletic (softball, basketball) scholarship. There's no way I could have done it on my own. College planning is just one of the many stressful times when young adults are looking ahead to their future. They might have the goal, but there are a lot of steps that go into actually following through with getting into college—as with any other major goal in life. But, if you enlist the help of a role model, mentor, or helper who really cares to see you succeed, you can accomplish the goal.

DO NOW! CREATE 101 WISHES

This exercise is inspired by *Dare to Win*. Canfield challenges his readers to actually write down a big list of 101 wishes. This helps you dream big and explode your goal-setting. When creating your list, come up with wishes that you could conceivably achieve—you're not going to be able to go back in time and hang out with dinosaurs. Your wishes should cross all of the Six Fs (Future, Fitness, Friendships, Family, Finances, and Fun). This activity stretches your imagination and opens your eyes and heart to future opportunity outside of your day-to-day living.

DO NOW! REVISIT A PAST GOAL

Grab your journal or a piece of paper. Write about a time in the past when you set a goal and you achieved it. What was the goal? What steps did you take? What challenges did you overcome? How did you feel when you achieved it? Take a minute to re-experience the good feelings that came from that success—and just think, you can have more of those good feelings every time you achieve one of your goals.

DO NOW! CREATE LONG-TERM AND SHORT-TERM GOALS

The choices you make *today* can take you closer to your dreams for the future. Use this "Do Now" as an opportunity to put yourself on the right path.

1. **Take out your journal or a piece of paper.** Create a list of long-term goal for each of the Six Fs: Future, Fitness, Friendships, Family, Finances, and Fun. Your long-term goals are the desires you feel in your gut. These are the goals you connect with on a deep level even if they're not something you can accomplish right now or all at once. Likely, daydreaming about these goals makes you feel a sense of exhilaration.

2. **Decide which of the long-term goals you can affect right now.** It's not possible to do everything all at once, so you have to prioritize based on current circumstances. For instance, maybe one of your long-term goals is to have kids. That's great, but it's not something you want to get

started on when you're in high school. So, you can write it down, but make a mental note to defer that particular long-term goal and keep it on the back burner or in your deep subconscious until you're older.

3. For each of the long-term goals that you want to pursue right now, create a short-term goal. Long-term goals are made up of dozens or hundreds of short-term goals. You have to chunk it down into bite-sized segments in order to make progress. These short-term goals should have a sense of urgency or an immediate energy. What can you get excited about doing right now? What can you do this week or this month to propel yourself toward your desired future?

DO NOW! HAVE A TABLE TALK ON GOAL-SETTING

Meet up with your friends and have a goal-setting brainstorming session. Help each other create 101 wishes. Ask family and friends: "What do you think are my skills or strengths?" Likely, they will have noticed something positive about you that perhaps you haven't noticed in yourself. We all have blind spots, so a good table talk will give you the chance to see yourself how others see you.

YOUNG ADULTS TALK ABOUT...MAKING THEIR GOALS A REALITY

"When I set goals, I set them really high—insanely high. Like, 'I want to climb a mountain in a day.' You just keep going at it and, before you know it, you're halfway there. That sounds cliché, but you just gotta keep going."

"For me, to be really motivated to do something, I have to know that it *can* happen. I picture it in my mind. If it seems too far out of reach, I give up on it. I have to know it's realistic."

"With any goal that I have, the thing I do is articulate it. If you have something you want to do, don't let it be a vague idea in your head. Write it down and say it exactly: this is what I'm going to do, this is how, and this is why. And then tell as many people as you can. It helps to say it aloud."

ACCEPT AND BELIEVE YOU CAN MAKE YOUR LIFE BETTER

What does it mean to "make life better"? Well, "better" can only be defined by you. Ask yourself—what would make your life better right now? Do you need to step up your physical fitness so you can have more energy and better body image? Would you like to have stronger bonds with your family or friends? Are you feeling like you could benefit from cultivating a stronger spiritual practice? "Better" depends on your completely unique perspective.

A better life starts with a better attitude. If you're wishing your life were better, there's a good chance that you're unhappy or frustrated with some aspect at the moment. That's okay. Acknowledge that reality and give yourself time to feel the way you're feeling. But don't stay in that negative place for too long, otherwise, feeling bad just becomes a habit. You can train yourself to believe that everything sucks, and you can wallow in misery and wander aimlessly with no motivation. Or, you can nudge yourself in a new and better direction and shake off the bad stuff.

Whichever attitude you choose, be aware that there's usually a domino effect—if you give up on one area in life, you might start giving up on other areas. I've seen this in students time and time again. They think they've dug themselves into a hole (even when they haven't), and it spirals out from there. They can be sixteen or seventeen years old—decades of life still ahead of them—and yet somehow convince themselves that life will never get better.

It is always possible to better your life. Even if you can't change your circumstances, you can choose a better outlook. But, it does require that you endure through the present moment and take the long view on life. "Better" is usually a gradual process.

A BETTER LIFE STARTS THE MOMENT YOU WAKE UP

Your best life starts the minute you get out of bed in the morning. Don't believe me? Try this: Imagine waking up and telling yourself that today is going to be terrible and tomorrow is going to be worse. Tell yourself that you're a failure and that you're never going to graduate from high school. Think about that—isn't it ridiculous? Speak it out loud and you'll see how irrational it is. Yet so many of us start the day by rehashing yesterday's problems and stressors, when we could be seeing each day as a fresh opportunity to make our life better.

You have the opportunity every single morning to shape your life into a masterpiece. If you want to excel in life, a good starting point is your physical well-being. You shape your day from the minute you get out of bed, and if you wake up feeling sluggish because you stayed up late playing video games the night before, well, that just makes it all the more difficult to start the day right. So, as basic as it sounds, if you want to dream big, that starts with treating your body well.

CREATING A VISION FOR YOUR FUTURE

If you want to make your life better, it starts with a vision. A fun way to imagine your better future is by creating a vision board. You can make one whenever you need to bust out of a rut or create a transition in your life. You can make an overall vision board including all of the Six Fs (Future, Fitness, Friendships, Family, Finances, and Fun) or you can focus in on one area of your life. Let's say you want to have better body image. You can do a whole vision board filled with inspiring, empowering images that will help you love your body more. This stimulates the mentality that you can make your life better.

To construct your vision board, get a large poster board and lots of inspiring imagery, which you can get from magazines, photos you've taken, or images you've printed out from online sources. You can also write out inspirational statements and put them on your board. Write it out as "I wish," "I want," or "I will." This is a forward-thinking activity, so don't use images or statements that relate to your past or present. Really try to visualize what you don't already have.

If you'd like, you can create your vision board using an online resources like Pinterest, or you can create your board in a digital program like Photoshop. If you create a digital collage, you can use your visionary imagery as the wallpaper on your phone or computer.

DO NOW! CREATE A VISION BOARD

Using the instructions in this chapter, choose one (or more) of the Six Fs (Future, Fitness, Friendships, Family, Finances, and Fun) and create a board that shows your vision of the ideal future. When you complete the process, put your vision board in a place that offers the opportunity to look at it in the morning and before bedtime. Focus on your images, feel the feelings they evoke, and imagine yourself having, being, or accomplishing whatever it is you envision for yourself.

YOUNG ADULT TALK ABOUT…
BELIEVING THEY HAVE THE POWER TO MAKE LIFE BETTER

"What I love about myself is the fact that I am able to pick myself back up. I am able to constantly evolve and change myself into the human being I strive to be. I love being able to transition my bad habits into better ones, because while we are not perfect, we are never our mistakes."

"When I quit a sport I had been involved with for five years, I became broken inside. I could feel the shards of my being falling apart. I didn't know who I would be outside of the sport. With time, lots of self-reflection, and a new list of goals,

I was able to move on and realize that taking time for oneself is incredibly important for growth. I can always return to that sport, but I'll only be a teenager once, and it is of the utmost importance that I build a strong, healthy relationship with myself now before I move into the 'real' world."

SEEK OUT ROLE MODELS AND MENTORS

Once you've identified your personal values and aspirations, you can find the role models who resonate with you. But this requires prioritizing your life. If you don't know what's most important to you, your eyes will not be open to seeing the people in your life who can help you go after it. The parents who love you. The teachers, counselors, and coaches who want to help you become the best you can be. That good friend who is lifting you up every single day. The spiritual leaders who can give you guidance. There are role models available in each domain of life. Even when you've got big goals, there are people in your life who have been there and done it. You can learn from their experience.

There are two types of role models—touchable and untouchable. Untouchable role models are those people you look up to even though you don't know them personally. For me, my untouchable role models are Jack Canfield, Oprah, and Ellen DeGeneres. Even though I'm not friends with them (...yet! Anything can happen in this life...), I admire their work and have grown immeasurably from it. Touchable role models are the people walking around in your everyday life. These can be parents, teachers, coaches, peers—anyone who models excellence. A mentor is a role model who takes it a step further—this is someone who actually works with you, usually one-on-one, to help you achieve your goals. A mentor is someone who is willing to take you under their wing and guide you.

My first role model and mentor was Craig Montag, the director at Brooklyn Park. I already spoke a bit earlier about the important role that Brooklyn Park played in my life. But there's more. When I was a kid, Craig was the most powerful, positive male influence in my life. I latched onto him and became his worker bee and sidekick, and I helped him in any way I could. He was very strict, and that was a good thing for me. He's a disciplinarian, but he also gives his heart. He changed my life. At my home, I was used to being disciplined, but it wasn't healthy discipline. It was violent, fear-based discipline, and I was usually very scared at home. What Craig offered was structure. I was afraid to disappoint him because I respected him so much, and it kept me in line. I wanted to make him proud.

What nobody at Brooklyn Park knew was that my life at home was the polar opposite of my life at the park. If I hadn't had the serendipity to have moved next to Brooklyn Park when I was young, and to have recognized Craig as an important role model, I wouldn't be who I am today. He was a father figure and my biggest fan, and he later became my friend and even my colleague, since I eventually became a park director with Craig after I graduated from high school. Craig made an impact on me, and he taught me how to impact others. That's why it's so crucial to keep your eyes open so that you can become aware of the many mentors and role models in your life, many of whom will gladly make themselves available to guide you. But it's up to you to pay attention and reach out. These people are right in front of you.

CHOOSE ROLE MODELS AND MENTORS WHO PUSH YOU TO BE YOUR BEST

Role models are not easy—they push you. The good *and* bad thing about mentorship is that your mentor takes you down from the clouds and puts you back down on planet earth. Their job is to point out the areas where you're not living up to your potential, and to point out your missteps. This can be tough. It can be an ego bruiser. But you've got to break past your inner resistance if you're to take in their feedback and let it direct you in a positive way.

When I was in high school, I was fortunate to have three strong women role models in athletics and academics: Linda McLellan (head volleyball coach, softball coach, and health/physical education teacher),

Katie Meyer (head softball coach and volleyball assistant coach), and Jan Watt (head of the *Clarion*, our school newspaper). These women are *tough*. They challenged me mentally and physically, and held me to strict standards of performance as both a student and an athlete.

As any Cleveland High School student or faculty member can attest, Jan never goes anywhere without her trademark purple pen. It's an extension of herself and a symbol of her commitment to keeping people accountable. In high school, Jan was my government and economics teacher. I was lucky, because I really accepted her philosophy and her pursuit of excellence. She has high expectations, and she's super candid, so if you don't meet her expectations, you're going to hear about it. I was sometimes scared and intimidated and really challenged by her "old school" mentality, but it made me feel safe because I knew what was expected of me, and I thrived within that dynamic. I knew Jan would be my biggest fan if I stepped up and did it right. She gives her students chances to succeed. When I wrote a paper, she marked it up with her purple pen and expected me to rewrite until I got it right. When I met her standards and got the A, it was like the heavens fell into my hands. Out of all four years in high school, the one class I took with Jan prepped me the most for college papers—the writing, research, comprehension, works cited. That has rippled out into my life. I wouldn't be writing this book if I hadn't had Jan as a role model and mentor.

Of course, role models and mentors are human, and you might find yourself coming into conflict with a mentor. That's okay. Conflict is natural in close relationships. What does matter is how you choose to address it. If your mentor pushes you in a way that bruises your ego, go ahead and feel that feeling privately. Don't indulge in a knee-jerk reaction. Then, later, if you need some clarification, approach your mentor when you're calm and ask questions in a respectful fashion. "Can you explain?" is always a good question. Remember, your mentor is a human being, trying their hardest. Have compassion for them and gratitude for the fact that they're putting their energy into helping you. Good mentors and role models can change your life.

YOUNG ADULTS TALK ABOUT...THEIR MENTORS AND ROLE MODELS

"My grandmother is my biggest inspiration. She founded an adoption agency and improves so many children's lives. I hope to be like her one day and to help people like she has."

"The most important influence in my life, outside of my family, is my ballet teacher. I have known her for over a decade and she has taught me not only how to be a better dancer, but how to be a better person as well. She's never given up on me, even when I lost faith in myself."

"My dad has always been a good influence when it comes to fitness. He makes me believe that I can always push myself to be better. He started taking me running with him when I was in the eighth grade and we bonded over it. Now, he's helping me train through a half marathon. I run track and cross-country, and I owe a lot of those accomplishments to him."

ALWAYS BE LOOKING FOR NEW ROLE MODELS AND MENTORS

When you're a goal-setter, you're likely to look for new challenges to replace the challenges you've already overcome. New challenges often necessitate finding new mentors. It's okay to outgrow and separate from a mentor. Learn from mentors, but don't get overly attached. This is good advice for adult life, too. Pay attention to the greatness that's around you, as the need for mentorship never stops.

DO NOW! WRITE A "THANK YOU" LETTER TO YOUR MENTOR OR ROLE MODEL

Write a heartfelt "thank you" letter to someone who has been a role model or mentor in your life. Try to be as specific as possible, letting them know exactly why you appreciate them. It feels good to be able to express appreciation for someone who has helped you, and he or she will undoubtedly cherish the letter.

Dear Linda McLellan,

When I first met you as my volleyball coach at Cleveland High School back when I was a freshman, my first reaction was "holy shit." Just from looking at you and seeing your confident, no-bull-shit demeanor, I knew you were serious business and that I'd better think before I spoke or acted. And I was right. Linda, you are a pillar of strength, and you were the disciplinarian I needed at the time. I am who I am today because of your high expectations, guidance, and your belief that motivated people can improve their life. Yes, I had the intrinsic motivation, but you reaffirmed my personal aspirations and held me accountable as my teacher, coach, role model, and mentor.

While I built a strong respect for you as a role model during my high school years, I also built a strong trust in you as a listener. I went to you often to share the details of my life. You listened attentively, and you helped me see that I couldn't change anyone but myself. You taught me that it was unrealistic to try to change my family dynamics, and that the only path I could take was to be my best self and lead by example. You pushed me to fight through hardship and go after my dreams. You always believed in me, and I owe much of my success to your example.

Linda, thank you for your strength and dedication, and for devoting yourself daily to your students. We are all blessed to know you.

Love,
Camille

YOUR THANKS ARE NEVER FORGOTTEN...

Since I've been teaching, I've had the good fortune to receive some "thank you" letters from past students. These truly touch my heart. I've include a few snippets here to show you that, if you do reach out and send a thoughtful letter to a role model in your life, they'll likely never forget you.

"When you came into my science class and pulled me out to tell me you want me to succeed, you simply changed my life. I have never had a person in my life believe in me like you do."

"Your leadership class taught me how to use my time efficiently and finish projects on time, but has also taught me how to be more open with friends and family, build stronger relationships, and be able to express how I am feeling to others verbally."

"As a coach, you have pushed me to limits I didn't know were possible, physically, mentally, and emotionally. You have shown me what it means to be on a team and how to be a team player. You have given me so much confidence. Although being your libero on the varsity volleyball team was probably the scariest thing I have ever done, you pushed me to be the best. The fact that you had so much faith in me made me believe the same within myself."

To read more stories and letters, visit ADANA Dynamics online at www.adanadynamics.com.

PART 4

NO NONSENSE

As you can probably imagine, as a high school teacher, I hear a lot of excuses from my students. But do you want to know which excuse is number one?

"I don't have a pencil."

Really think about that. These are kids who are effectively saying, "I can't go forward with this goal because I don't have a pencil." Seriously? Pencils aren't exactly difficult to get ahold of. You can always turn around and ask a friend. So, if you're going to let a damn pencil hold you back, then I honestly can't help you.

If you want to create the life you're dreaming of, you've got to cultivate a "no nonsense" approach to life. This means taking 100 percent accountability for yourself. Period. It means not making excuses. When you're in class, your focus should be on academics—and that means having the proper tools for the job. When you complain to a teacher that you don't have a pencil, what you communicate is that you are not prepared and you're willing to make excuses for yourself.

Of course, sometimes life interrupts, and we honestly do have a legitimate excuse for dropping the ball on something. If you're experiencing an illness or there's a death in the family, of course you need to give yourself some leeway. You're a human being, not a robot. Otherwise, though, no matter your circumstances—socioeconomic status, learning challenges, and so on—you *learn* to make excuses. It's a habit. And if you surround yourself with other excuse-makers, you might be feeling pretty comfortable and warm in your excuse-nest.

When I'm in the classroom and I'm hearing these kinds of lame excuses, I put my students on blast. But since I can't multiply myself and come put you on blast in person, it's up to you to cultivate this no-nonsense attitude for yourself. Please, though, understand that I do this with love, and I encourage you to cultivate a love-based no-nonsense attitude. You're going to stumble—we all do. It's okay. I'm not saying that you should create unreasonable expectations for yourself and beat yourself up when you don't meet them. Be loving and compassionate with yourself, but also challenge yourself. That's the no-nonsense approach.

SPEND TIME WITH QUALITY PEOPLE

We spend most of our lives surrounded by people—family, friends, classmates, teammates, coworkers. There's no shortage in terms of quantity. But what about quality? That can be harder to find. But if you want to achieve your goals, you have to surround yourself with high-quality people. This means evaluating those in your life and asking some tough questions: Does that person have goals that they're actively working toward? Do they have good judgment? Are they kind and uplifting? Are they supportive and communicative?

Unfortunately, you'll likely find that not everyone in your life has these good qualities. That's okay. It doesn't mean you have to judge them or drop them. However, it does mean you can choose to be different. Since I witnessed firsthand the effects of alcoholism and drug use in my family, I chose friends that weren't partaking, because I knew it wasn't a dynamic I wanted in my life. I had friends who started using drugs and alcohol, and even though I tried to talk to them about it, I knew I couldn't change them. That's okay. It just meant that I was able to connect with them on some levels and not others. I could hang out with those people during class or extracurriculars, but not during the times when they were partying.

The good news is that when you start to discern who in your life is a quality person, you will find them. They're there, just waiting to be recognized and appreciated. When you have a gut feeling that a person is high quality, put yourself out there to spend time with them. Be proactive about it. Put in the time to make that relationship fun and engage with someone who shares the same values and aspirations that you do.

HEALTHY RELATIONSHIPS HAVE HEALTHY BOUNDARIES

Motivational speaker Jim Rohn said, "The greatest gift you can give to somebody is your own personal development. I used to say, 'If you will take care of me, I will take care of you.' Now I say, 'I will take care of me for you if you will take care of you for me.'"

What exactly does this mean? It means that each of us must come to our relationships as a whole, healthy person. We cannot expect the other person to supply us with something we lack. No one can "make you" feel beautiful, confident, worthwhile, intelligent, or anything else for that matter. You have to cultivate those qualities within yourself. That way, when you do enter into relationship with someone—be that a parent, teacher, friend, or sweetheart—you can create good boundaries and separate yourself from them. Try this: hold your two hands up in front of you. Make two firsts and press them together, knuckle to knuckle. Now, pull your fists away from each other. See how easily they come apart? Each fist is whole, and separates cleanly and easily from the other. That's a healthy relationship—you can come together, but still maintain your individuality. Now, hold up your hands again, this time intertwining your fingers. Hold on tight and try to pull your hands apart. There's more resistance. This is what it's like in a codependent relationship—where there's too much interdependence, too much clinging between two people. That's when neediness and jealousy come into the picture, because neither person is operating independently as a whole, healthy person.

Quality people do not want to be in an unhealthy, codependent relationship with you. And what's more, they've done their *own* personal development so that they know what unhealthy relationships look like, and they actively avoid them.

REACH OUT TO LIKE-MINDED GOAL SETTERS

When you're in high school or college, it can be easy to get locked into your friend group. But likely, if you look around you, there are people out there who you admire and who'd make a great connection for you. Remember to reach out. If you have an instinct about someone's character and think they'd be good for you, go for it. If you sense a connection with a fellow goal-setter, say hello, get a conversation going. It can feel vulnerable, but it can be worthwhile. You might find yourself with an amazing connection.

When I was in high school and trying to perfect my shot in basketball, I'd partner up with a friend. I'd shoot and she'd rebound, and then we'd flip and I'd rebound for her. It was fun and social, and I was able to make an observation of someone else's skill, which gave me feedback that I could use in building my own skills. When you work with a quality person who shares your goals, it can be fun and increase your motivation.

DO NOW! FIND AN ACTIVITY BUDDY

When you have a passion or hobby, it can be fun to make it social. Take a couple minutes to think about who in your life could be an activity buddy. Could you play a sport together? Do crafts? Make music? Reach out right now and invite them.

FRIENDS FOR A REASON, A SEASON, AND A LIFETIME

Common wisdom says that we have three types of friends: friends for a reason, friends for a season, and friends for a lifetime. What this means is that friends and sweethearts cycle in and out of your life. Perhaps you're friends because you're in the same class, but when the class ends, you don't have a "reason" to hang out anymore. That's okay. Perhaps you have a best friend in high school, but you may not be close after you graduate as your lives naturally take different paths. That's okay too. People grow and change through the seasons of their life, and it's okay if some friendships expire.

The hope, though, is that you can cultivate at least a few friendships that stick. True friends are rare, and you never know when you're going to meet one. I met my best friend, Josie, in Spanish class. It was the silliest moment: I was sitting on the other side of the classroom. We made eye contact, and she faked as if she were flicking a booger at me. So, I faked back—pretending like I'd caught the booger. We were instant best friends. Not only do we have fun together, but she and her family were an incredible influence on my life. Her family took me in, cared for me, fed me, and showed me a family life that I couldn't experience in my own house. All through high school, I only had one best friend. Sure, I had friends in my classes and on my sports teams and from Brooklyn Park, but Josie was THE most amazing friend—and still is to this day, because she loves me, believes in my dreams, and holds me accountable. When you choose to only surround yourself with quality people, you'll likely find that you have fewer friends, but quality outweighs quantity.

DO NOW! CRAFT A GOAL-SETTING CARD

This "Do Now" is a fun, crafty way to create and share goals, and enlist the help of friends in holding you accountable. For this activity, you need a greeting card, goals, and a friend or two (or more). First, write up at least one goal in each of the Six Fs (Future, Fitness, Friendships, Family, Finances, and Fun). Next, get a greeting card. You and your friends can have a craft party where you make cards together, or you can go to a store and purchase one. When your card is ready, write down the goals you created and then trade cards with your friends so that everyone walks away with someone else's card. Hold on to the card (make sure to put it in a safe place) and schedule a time to check back in and revisit those goals together. This creates extrinsic accountability.

DO NOW! JOURNAL ABOUT THE QUALITY PEOPLE IN YOUR LIFE

Grab your journal or a piece of paper, and create a list of the quality people in your life. In what ways are they quality? Do they support your goals? Do they lift you up? Do they compliment you? Do they listen to you?

DO NOW! WRITE A LOVE LETTER TO A QUALITY PERSON IN YOUR LIFE

When you have quality people in your life, let them know! Don't be shy. Everyone loves to hear that they've been a positive influence in someone's life. Write a letter to show your love and appreciation.

YOUNG PEOPLE TALK ABOUT...QUALITY PEOPLE IN THEIR LIVES

"My uncle is one of the most inspiring people in my life because he helped define creativity for me. I grew up always thinking I was less creative than my brother, but my uncle taught me that creativity does not have to be one way. That changed my life."

"My family and friends have created a truly safe and supportive environment for me to grow up in, where I can feel free of judgment, build my self-confidence, and become more of a trusting person."

"One time I had a major essay due and I was feeling unmotivated because I didn't feel like I knew what I was doing. It wasn't that I was lazy. I just felt like I wasn't smart enough. My best friend was writing the same essay and was under the same stress, and still chose to take the time to help me and support me. I ended up being able to finish the essay and have something I was proud of."

"Be with people who make you the best possible version of you. Don't let people poison you with negativity. Life it too short to let them take any of the good away from you."

THINK ABOUT DECISION-MAKING AND POSSIBLE OUTCOMES

Your life can change in a split second. As a teacher, I go to funerals way too often for students who have passed away too young, often due to reckless circumstances. You owe it to your loved ones to have care for what you do in your decision-making. Think forward to how much your decisions affect the people in your life. I do think, as human beings, we need to learn from our mistakes, but too often people repeat the same mistake over and over again. This can be avoided if you take the time to practice your decision-making skills and learn to choose the positive outcome.

EVENT + RESPONSE = OUTCOME

Jack Canfield has an equation called E + R = O. That stands for "Event Plus Response Equals Outcome." This is a decision-making process that you can use to think forward to the possible consequences of your actions. For example, let's say that the event was a school project, and your response was to wait until the last minute. Because you procrastinated, you became overwhelmed and couldn't complete the project on time. So, the outcome is that you earn a zero on the school project, which affects your grade and maybe even your eligibility to graduate or get into your first-choice college. Now that you know that those are the possible negative outcomes, you can change your response and alter the future for the better.

Here's another example. If you go to a party, get drunk, and decide to drive, what are all the possible outcomes? You hit someone. Someone hits you. You kill your best friend in the passenger seat. You get pulled over. You lose your license. You get fined. You go to jail. There are so many potentially terrible outcomes to this scenario. If you can perform this equation quickly and use your imagination to generate possible scenarios, you'll instinctively say "Nope!" That's because you realize there are more potential negative outcomes than positive ones. Since substances cloud your judgment, it's best to practice E + R = O before the party begins—and share your plan with a friend who can help hold you accountable to it.

This equation applies to all decision-making scenarios. You want to have sex, but the guy doesn't want to use a condom—what are the possible outcomes? A friend wants to get high before school starts—what are the possible outcomes? When you really think it through, you can quickly generate a response that is good for you in the long run. Decision-making is a skill that can be practiced.

YOUNG ADULTS TALK ABOUT...MAKING GOOD DECISIONS

"I only feel comfortable taking risks when I'm with the people who have the same values as me."

"Last year I had a teacher who was going through a rough time in his life like I was. My mom and I were on very bad terms and fighting any time we spoke. One day, my teacher pulled me aside and said, 'Look, things are rough for us both, but you're an excellent student and I know I'm a decent teacher. I know you can finish school on time, unlike I did. Just keep going.' Every day I think about what he'd expect of me. When I half-ass something, I think about how he'd grade me. If I don't like it, I do better."

"My friends keep me in line. When I ask to hang out, they say, 'what about your homework?' Or they say, 'I'm not so sure we should do that' when I think of crazy ideas."

MAKING GOOD DECISIONS AT EVERY STAGE OF LIFE

Decision-making changes depending on your stage of life. As a high school teacher, I get to see the huge changes that students go through between freshman and senior years. First-year students don't have the same concerns as seniors, who are transitioning into adulthood. And that's perfectly normal. But it doesn't mean you can't have a goal that you're working toward *now*. Juniors and seniors might be looking at more weighty decisions, but freshmen and sophomores are laying important groundwork. No matter your stage in life, you can set goals and work right now to meet them. If you're a freshman, you might be more concerned about finding your community, figuring out what sports you want to play or what clubs you want to join. This is a relatively small goal; if you don't choose the "right" club in you first year, that's okay—that's just part of the exploratory process of life. It's okay to make some missteps. It's good practice for when you're a couple years older and you're making weightier decisions—like when you're a junior or senior and you're trying to figure out if you want to go on to college or if you want to find a job after graduation.

MAKE GOOD DECISIONS NOW...REAP THE REWARDS LATER

Later on in the book we'll be discussing the concept of delayed gratification. But I'd like to introduce it here, since you can make your best decisions *now* if you think about the payoff in the future. Let's say you're playing video games and you know in the back of your mind that you've got a goal that needs accomplishing. Can you truly enjoy the video game, or is there a niggling anxiety at the back of your brain? This makes you feel bad about yourself, because you know in your heart that you're making a poor decision in the moment. And if your self-esteem plummets, that creates a ripple effect into other areas of your life. Instead, make the right decision in the moment—in this case, by working toward your goal *first*—and then, once you've worked hard, you can fully relax and enjoy the video game because you know deep down that you deserve it.

DO NOW! CREATE TEN COMMITMENTS

If you want to make good decisions, you first have to know what you value and what you expect of yourself. Create a list of ten commitments you want to make to yourself. These commitments can be targeted toward different areas—you can create ten commitments related to drugs and alcohol; ten commitments about relationships, love, and sex; ten commitments toward academics and the future. When you find yourself needing to make a decision, you can check in with yourself: "Is this choice in alignment with my ten commitments to myself?" Taking the time to reflect, analyze, and create personal commitments teaches you how to reject the distractions and negative influences around you.

DO NOW! E + R = O

Grab your journal or a piece of paper, and find a quiet place to be alone with your thoughts. Think back to past situation in which you didn't make a good decision. Be really honest with yourself. It's just you and your journal—there's no one to judge you. Then, think through all the possible responses and outcomes. With the benefit of hindsight, you can likely see what the best response would have been. You can use this insight going forward the next time you're faced with a decision.

CHOOSE OPTIMISM

First of all, I want you to notice that the title of this chapter is "Choose Optimism." *Choose* it. Of course, some people have a naturally sunny disposition and are predisposed to see the glass half full. And then, of course, there are people who suffer from clinical depression or anxiety. For the rest of us, though, we're likely somewhere in between—we *could* be more optimistic, but we're not actively choosing it. If you want to pursue and achieve your goals in life, that orientation absolutely has to change.

Optimism requires mental fortitude. It's hard to be optimistic when so many of us are suffering from hardships and stress. So, when you meet a person who exudes optimism, you should have a lot of respect for that, because likely that person works hard to keep shifting their perspective on life and seeing the upside. It's easy to wallow in negativity. But when you do, it doesn't just affect you; it brings other people down too. Optimism and pessimism are both contagious, so you if you want to have a positive impact on the people in your life, you have to get mentally tough and learn how to pull yourself up.

My cousins Melissa and Sabrina and their mother, my aunt Rachel, are some of the most optimistic people I know. Every time we get together, no matter the circumstance, they bring in genuine optimism, laughter, and happiness. We all grew up together, with very similar family dynamics, and my cousins and I all lost our fathers and our grandmothers at the same time. So, they've known hardship. And yet they have a joy and vibrant energy that is contagious. It's impossible to be in a bad mood in their presence. That's why it's not only important to choose optimism, but to surround yourself with people that do so as well.

OPTIMISM IS A SUCCESS HABIT

Optimism and success go hand-in-hand. When you set a big goal for yourself, there will likely be moments when your mood or motivation are low and the process seems like a chore. When this happens, it's up to us to choose to see those responsibilities in an optimistic light or a negative one. Let's say you're in a running program. Yes, you can go for a run and hate every minute of it and feel like a ton of bricks. Or, you can go out there and choose optimism, which will make you automatically feel lighter. It's totally up to you. If it's something you have to get done—homework, practice, chores, or whatever—it's 100 percent your choice whether you go in with an optimistic attitude and enjoy it, or go in with a bad attitude and make it that much harder. That doesn't change the fact that you still have to do it.

People who choose optimism are much more likely to approach life with enthusiasm and a good work ethic. They take steps in the directions of their dreams and goals, and they accumulate mini successes along the way. This is a rush—and it'll make you want to replicate the feeling by achieving more and more success. But it all starts with practicing optimism and really making a habit of it so you can tap into it and experience its benefits.

The more you practice optimism, the more it becomes a habit, which makes it very easy to tap into and benefit from. You can make choices based on what you know makes you happy. That creates an upward spiral, with good choices leading to more good choices. Every single time you make a choice that makes you happy, it adds up. That's why it's meaningful and rewarding to make positive choices and do the right thing. You'll get either rewarded externally, or you can have the inner satisfaction, which is its own reward.

If you don't choose optimism, you limit your chances for success. Pessimistic people are likely to be stagnant or aimless, and as a result are more likely to feel fearful, out of control, and lacking in self-confidence.

These negative emotions then lead to more stagnation and aimlessness. Many people live life this way. You have to continually make the choice to guide yourself in a direction of choosing happiness. It's a simple concept, but easy to forget.

CHOOSING OPTIMISM WHEN YOU'RE DEPRESSED

It's one thing to be optimistic when things are going well. It's harder to keep a positive attitude when you're in the midst of hardship. Everyone experiences depression, whether it's clinical depression or just feeling down from time to time. Myself, I've gone through major depression. I get what it's like and how difficult it is. But when I tapped into happiness and optimism, that choice impacted me and those around me. Every human will experience a period of depression, and I believe we should embrace these and use them as times to reflect. Reflection allows for digging deep and breaking the repetitive cycles of negativity we're in. One of the ways I dug out of depression was by amping up my fitness level. Exercise pushed refresh on my endorphins, which then led to me feeling inspired to write in a journal and read books on personal development. When you're depressed, you can start with a single choice that makes you happier, and build from there.

OPTIMISM BRIGHTENS EVEN THE HARDEST TIMES

My grandmother's philosophy in her later years was "don't worry, be happy." Even when she was in hospice care, living out her last days, unable to move or take care of herself, she had an optimistic spirit. This was after a lifetime of being a big go-getter—she raised kids and worked hard, no matter what hardships and stress she endured, including the loss of three of her six children as well as three male partners. Her childhood and adulthood were packed with adversity and she overcame all the obstacles and still maintained a very positive attitude. At the end of her life, she lay in bed, belting out the song "Don't Worry, Be Happy" at the top of her lungs.

This was a beautiful moment for me, one I'll never forget. Even though I'm a huge goal-setter and I see the beauty in striving for the future, at the same time I can see the beauty in living in the moment and not worrying about outcomes you can't control. This was the lesson I took from my grandma the day before she died. You can strategize your life and set goals, but you should also balance that by being happy in the moment and with what you have. No matter your circumstance, there is good in it—you just have to choose to see it.

DO NOW! SURROUND YOURSELF WITH INSPIRATION

Find optimistic quotations and put them up in places that are visible to you—your bathroom mirror, your bedroom wall, your binder, your journal, as a screen saver on your phone or computer. Read them and absorb the message. When those quotes lose their freshness, switch them out for new ones.

DO NOW! TAKE IN THE GOOD

This practice is borrowed from neuropsychologist Dr. Rick Hanson, author of *Hardwiring Happiness*. Neuropsychologists study the ways our physical brain structure affects our psychology and state of mind. Hanson developed a practice called "taking in the good," which is a simple and radically effective mindfulness practice. Try it now:

1. Have a positive experience (or remember one)

2. Enrich it—really focus on it for twenty to thirty seconds.

3. Absorb it—imagine the positive experience absorbing into your body and soul.

DO NOW! SEE YOURSELF IN THE FUTURE

This exercise is inspired by Shawn Achor, who is an expert in the psychology of positivity and author of *The Happiness Advantage*. Use photo editing software like Photoshop to create a vision of your future self. Take a current photo of yourself and do your best to create an age progression. Try to create a photo of what you'll look like as a happy adult in your thirties. This is a great activity to show yourself that today isn't the end of the story—you have so much ahead of you to look forward to.

YOUNG ADULTS TALK ABOUT...BEING OPTIMISTIC

"I love that I see the good in the world rather than focusing on the evil. Many say I'm just overly positive and optimistic, but I truly believe everyone has the power to be great. If you set your mind to anything, you can accomplish it."

"I have a positive personality and I try to be happy all the time. I want my happiness to radiate off of me and onto other people."

PAY ATTENTION TO YOUR RESPONSES

When I was in high school, I made fun of a kid in my class for having bad breath. Then, that weekend, he died by drowning in the ocean—a wave took him away from his twin sister and that was it, he was dead. And my last memory of the guy was that I'd said something terrible to him. He hadn't done a thing to me. I was just trying to fit in with my friends in the classroom. I was frustrated that day because I wasn't able to sit at the table with my friends, and my reaction was to take it out on him.

It took me a long time to forgive myself for that one. And it taught me two lessons. The first being, of course, not to make fun of anyone. The second one being that it was up to me, and me alone, to avoid knee-jerk reactions. If I hadn't opened my mouth during a moment of frustration, I wouldn't have said something regrettable. The fact is, quick reactions are only good in sports or in true emergency situations. Otherwise, quick reactions usually do more harm than good. In this chapter, we'll differentiate between reactive responses and reflective responses, and explore ways to respond to circumstances and people from a healthy place.

REACTIVE RESPONSE VS. REFLECTIVE RESPONSE

We've all heard it: treat others the way we want to be treated. It's a simple, timeless piece of wisdom that is easier said than done. We're part of the human community, interacting with people on a daily basis, and the fact is...sometimes, we react. If something happens that hurts or offends us, we have that initial knee-jerk response. We get defensive, angry, scared, shocked, sad. That's human nature. But it's worth learning how to manage those responses, because if you act from that reactive place, you're likely to just amplify the original problem and create new ones. This can interrupt life, derail your goals, and create problems in your important relationships.

Instead, what you want is a reflective response—one that is calm, cool-headed, and geared toward accepting or improving the situation. This means that, yes, you feel your feelings and you process through them. If someone hurts you, feel hurt. That's okay. But when it comes to choosing how to respond to that situation, take some time to reflect. Check in with the HALT acronym and make sure you're not reacting from a place of being hungry, angry, lonely, or tired. Go through the "Event + Response = Outcome" decision-making process we talked about in the chapter titled "Think about Decision-Making and Possible Outcomes." Your responses point directly to what is most meaningful to you in your life.

For instance, let's say you're driving and someone cuts you off. Of course, you're going to have an immediately physiological reaction and your adrenaline is going to be pumping. But what happens after that is up to you. Do you get instantly enraged? Do you scream at them and flip the bird? Do you spend the rest of your drive pissed off at that other driver? Okay, well think about it—what else could you have been doing with that precious time and energy? If you spend it on road rage, then at some level you're giving anger—a negative and temporary emotion—a place of importance in your life. That's going to detract from your emotional well-being and your ability to focus on achieving your goals. Instead, let's say that same driver cuts you off—and you shrug and let it go. That's a way of affirming to yourself that you've got your priorities straight and you're not going to let someone else's unconscious actions distract you from living and feeling the way you want to. That's just one scenario, but you can approach all of life in this thoughtful manner.

RESPONDING TO LIFE'S FEEDBACK

People and situations are going to give you feedback whether you want them to or not. If you get a poor grade, that's feedback that you need to work harder to understand the material. If you make a sarcastic joke to a friend and it hurts their feelings, that's feedback that you need to be gentler with them. Maybe you post something to social media and you get trolled with nasty comments—that's the kind of feedback that none of us wants.

No matter the content and source of the feedback, it's an opportunity to analyze your influences. This can help you figure out what feedback to take in and what to dismiss.

Who is the source of this feedback? Is it coming from a friend or family member who genuinely knows you and wants to keep you accountable to being your best self? Are they a healthy, thoughtful person who has your best interests in mind? If so, they're probably worth listening to. You should let quality people speak, and take that in. Or, is the feedback coming from someone who you've observed as having a tendency to be hypercritical, judgmental, or negative? We've all heard the phrase "haters are gonna hate," and it's actually true. When someone is predisposed to pessimism, they're going to filter their opinions through that mindset. That's not to say that you can't take away something valuable from their feedback, but it does mean that you should be wary. This is just another case for analyzing your influences.

If a quality person, someone you've chosen to spend time with, has taken the time to see you and hear you, and to cultivate feedback for you, that's a gift. They didn't have to spend their time thinking about you and wanting to help you improve yourself. Thank them for taking the time to consider you. If you're really hearing what people are telling you—as opposed to being reactive, resistant, or defensive—then you can really identify what person might be saying. Compassionate listening is

the act of being a sponge. You soak up what the other person is saying—
you really take it in, without being judgmental or defensive.

A YOUNG ADULT TALKS ABOUT...HEARING FEEDBACK

"I take criticism and use it to fuel me as motivation. I am confident and not afraid to fail."

WHAT DO YOUR RESPONSES SAY ABOUT YOU?

The way you respond to others is directly related to how you feel about
yourself. When you're paying attention, you can treat your responses
as measuring sticks to gauge your levels of self-esteem and figure out
whether you're providing enough care for yourself. Reactions are often
based in unresolved feelings: we're dealing with something internally
that we haven't shared or voiced. That's when people lash out. For
example, if you see someone else who has achieved a goal and you feel
jealous of them, it's important to realize that the jealousy may stem
from your own insecurity about where you are in life. You can ask
yourself, "Why am I jealous? Is it because I feel like I'm not accomplishing my goals and I don't feel like I have anything to be proud of?"
Or, if you find yourself feeling irritable or argumentative with the
important people in your life, you can check in: "Am I taking care of
myself so that I can show up as my best self to my family and friends?
Do I need to get some extra sleep? Do I need to cut down on the caf-
feine and junk food?"

When you choose healthy, calm responses, you tell the people in your
life that you care about them and yourself. When I was in high school,
I used to be very reactive and defensive, because I was dealing with so
much in my life. My best friend, Josie, was the polar opposite. She has a
very yoga-like approach to life. She accepts what comes and flows with

it. This is part of why we formed such a strong friendship, because her energy balanced mine. Her lack of negative reactions was (and still is) her way of hugging me, and her calm nature has always felt very safe to me. One of the most beautiful things you can give someone else is a sense of safety, and she was my security blanket for a long time—all because she was very calm with her responses.

When you choose to respond to life from a place of reflection rather than reaction, the benefits are two-fold: you take care of yourself, and you strengthen your bonds with your loved ones. This is a gift you can give to all of the people in your life—yourself included.

DO NOW! FREE WRITE YOUR REACTIONS

Grab your journal. Is there something that's bothering you? It's normal to react emotionally when you're hurt, angry, or disappointed. This exercise can help you process those feelings without doing damage to yourself or your important relationships. "Free write" for ten minutes without stopping. It doesn't matter what you say or if you contradict yourself. Just go. React. Let it out. This is a safe space to get out those uncensored feelings without hurting anyone.

DO NOW! DISSIPATE THE ENERGY

If you find yourself in a reactive mode, find a physical activity that helps dissipate the energy. Punch a pillow, go for a run—anything to burn off that negative energy in a healthy way.

DO NOW! REFLECT ON FEEDBACK YOU'VE RECEIVED

Take out your journal or a piece of paper. Who is in your life who challenges your perspective? Who constantly and consistently gives you specific, critical, guiding feedback? In your journal, create a T-chart. Label one side "positive" and the other "negative." Now, create a list of both the positive and negative emotions that come up for you when you're receiving feedback.

Now, take some time to reflect on how this person (or people) could ultimately help you in the long run. What can you take from their feedback? How does their feedback change your identity, personality, or beliefs about yourself?

PART 5

ACCOUNTABILITY

You've acknowledged your current reality, dealt with it, aspired, and taken a no-nonsense attitude with yourself. Now, to protect everything you've worked so hard to cultivate, you need to maintain accountability to yourself and your dreams.

Accountability is difficult. But it's only through accountability that you actually propel yourself forward and see the real benefits and results of all your hard work. And when you follow through, believe me, you'll feel a rush of euphoria. It's not a feeling that can be explained—you just have to go after it and experience it for yourself. And once you do, you'll want to re-create the experience, and that will make it that much easier to keep yourself accountable. With practice, accountability becomes a habit.

There are two types of accountability: internal and external. When you're motivated from within, your internal sense of accountability kicks in because you're naturally inspired to honor those expectations you've set for yourself. Internal accountability doesn't depend on you being held accountable by an outside force. Ideally, you should try to hold yourself accountable before you look to an outside source of accountability. But, of course, it can also be handy to have an accountability partner. This can be a role model, mentor, a member of your mastermind group (which is a group of people who have similar intentions to take steps toward their aspirations)—really, anybody who knows you have goals and wants to help you succeed.

At the end of the day, you are 100 percent accountable to your own choices—I hope you'll make the choices that support your best life.

EXPECT THE BEST

When I started hanging out at Brooklyn Park as a kid, it was my first real exposure to rules and expectations. You had to check out games and equipment before you used them. If you wanted to join the activities, you had to sign up on the chalkboard. If you wanted to play at the park, you had to abide by the rules set forth by the park director, Craig Montag.

Craig was *strict*. I'll never forget the time I used profanity while playing a game of ping pong. Craig stopped me and said, "Camille, you just lost the game automatically. You need to go sit at the picnic table behind the shack. I'll be there in a few." Thirty minutes later—which felt like an eternity!—Craig came by with a pen and paper and made me write 100 sentences. It was something like "I will never use bad language. It is disrespectful and not ladylike." I was only in middle school, but this experience created a profound shift within me. Though at the time I was sad that I'd disappointed Craig and afraid that he would stop caring about me, he had really done me a huge favor by creating structure, accountability, and a reprimand that I needed.

When the people in our life expect us to maintain high standards for ourselves, we have two choices: become defensive and angry, or flourish under the structure and support. I chose to flourish. With Craig as my guide, I learned to respect adults, maintain high standards for myself, and apologize for my actions when I stepped out of line.

EXPECT THE BEST FOR YOURSELF

When it comes to expecting the best, you must distinguish between what you can control and what you can't. You can *hope* that someone else does something, but you can't make it so. If you say, "I expect my mom or dad to do such-and-such," you're just setting yourself up for disappointment. You can't place expectations on others. You can only set expectations for yourself. For instance, you can say, "I'd *like* mom or dad to do such-and-such, but if they don't, then *I expect myself* to handle the disappointment calmly." If you expect someone else to make you happy, you're basing your happiness on the actions of another. How likely is it that he or she will treat you in exactly the way that will "make" you happy? Not very. But, if you cultivate happiness within yourself—a happiness that is independent of other people in the world—you've created a high expectation that *is* within your power to meet.

WHAT IF...

Some people think, "Always expect the worst and you'll never be disappointed." But that's not my perspective. I say, expect the best, but if something doesn't pan out the way you want it to or the way it "should," that's when you call on your healthy coping skills. It's very difficult when something doesn't turn out the way you expect, but that's not a cue to give up. That's when you turn to your skills in switching your perception of a hard reality. Or you reassure yourself that everything happens for a reason. Disappointments are a hard fact of life, but their inevitability does not mean that you need to lower your standards. It could mean that life has something better for you.

SURROUND YOURSELF WITH OTHERS WHO EXPECT THE BEST

With Craig Montag, I had a person in my life who expected the best of himself and of me. You too can find such people in your life. One way is to gather a mastermind group. This is a collection of likeminded goal-setters who have dreams or similar interests. It's a comfortable group setting (two or more people) where each member can talk through their passions and goals. Group members offer each other feedback, support, and accountability, and working in a social aspect adds an element of fun. You multiply your dreams when you surround yourself with your mastermind group.

I have a friend, Kendra Gardner, who is my accountability buddy. Both of us are goal-setters who like to think big, and we get a lot out of helping each other follow through on our goals. When I share a goal with Kendra, she gets excited for me. She says, "Okay, let's go. Let's do it. What are your steps?" And vice versa. She's a big thinker and dreamer. She tells me what she's thinking about and processing, and I help her go after it. We check in with each other once or twice a week to track our progress and cheer each other on. It's a great reciprocal relationship.

Relationships like these can be a fantastic source of challenge and compassion. Your accountability buddies should push you to be your best and be there to pick you up when you stumble.

YOUNG ADULTS TALK ABOUT...
WHAT MOTIVATES THEM TO BE THEIR BEST

"I play club baseball and on my team there are all these guys who are older than me. Some of them are going to great baseball schools. That's what I want, and I feel powerful when I'm surrounded by all these guys because I know that it's attainable."

"I stay excited about what I'm doing. I taught myself to play guitar and I kept up my excitement so that I could do it over and over again, even when I was messing up—it didn't matter."

"My father introduced me to running. He awakened my drive. I love running now, and I keep pushing myself further and further and it makes me feel good."

DO NOW! REFLECT ON ACCOUNTABILITY PARTNERS

Who do you get your accountability from? Yourself? A coach? A parent or guardian? Take time to reflect on this. When you're finished processing, get those people involved in your process. Do not hide it. Reveal it and honor the accountability around you. If you are internally accountable, keep the vision everywhere and look at it constantly.

DELAY GRATIFICATION

When you delay gratification, you give up a short-term reward in favor of one that is longer-term but much more fulfilling. For instance, if you're saving money to buy a car (a long-term goal), then you'll choose to stay home on Friday night instead of spending money going out to a movie with friends. If you're looking to lose weight (another long-term goal), you'll opt out of ordering the venti mocha with extra whipped cream at Starbucks—even though it would taste delicious *right now*. When you take a mindset of delaying gratification, you make decisions in the now that support the big goals you're working toward for the future.

We talked in earlier chapters about setting goals and expecting the best from yourself. Delaying gratification is just another facet of the process. It's not that you're depriving yourself in the moment, it's that you love yourself enough to see the moment as just a tiny part of life. It's that you've turned up the burning desire. You've turned up the flame in your heart and you'll do what it takes—you'll endure every single step—to accomplish your goal.

WHAT'S YOUR DESIRED END RESULT?

It takes some time to figure out what you want and to know why you're delaying gratification. And what "gratification" means will mean something different to everyone. If you're young and at the start of your journey, your end goals are naturally going to be different than someone who is older and more experienced. But, you're never too young to cultivate small or incremental goals. This can be based on any of the Six Fs: Future, Fitness, Friendships, Family, Finances, and Fun. If you're successful, this is going to blossom into self-love, and you'll send that love into the world. Ask yourself if you're willing to take the step to get to whatever the goal is. If you're willing to take the step, you're willing to delay gratification.

When you know what you want, you can visualize the outcome and almost rehearse it in your mind. If you do that enough, you fill your mind with your goals instead of getting distracted by this moment's shiny object and forgetting what you're trying to accomplish. For me, this focus started at a young age; I played two sports on average during each season and maintained high grades. This wasn't easy, and there were plenty of people around me who thought I needed to chill out and relax. But I was able to keep my focus because I knew I had to graduate high school and go on to college if I was going to break the patterns of my upbringing and forge the good life I wanted. Because I had a goal and I wanted it so fiercely, I could stay on track.

SHORT-TERM THINKING VS. LONG-TERM THINKING

This moment matters. When you're young—especially in high school— you can hear some contradictory messages: either you hear that this time in your life is unimportant and doesn't matter. Or that it's the *most* important time, so you'd better not screw it up. Well, which one is it? As is the case with everything in life, it's a balancing act. Do things in moderation. You can live in the moment, but don't let those moments become an addiction. If you've prioritized your life, you can keep focused on your long-term goal.

Having taught in a high school for so many years, I've seen the dilemma of short-term thinking play out over and over in the romantic lives of my students. Let's say you have a personal commitment to only have sex with someone you really love. Then, in high school, you fall in love, you have a major attraction, and one of you wants to have sex. But if you want an emotional attachment, you need to get past that initial rush and take the time to get to know that person. One person might want just a sexual relationship while the other wants something more. The one who wants more is broken-hearted when things don't work out. If you're pining over a romantic interest for six months, what do you think is going to happen to your schoolwork? Yep, it's going to go straight to hell. While sexual desires are natural and healthy, when you're in high school, becoming sexually active might be more trouble than it's worth. What if, during that six months when you're nursing a broken heart, your grades drop. And because of your poor grades, you don't get into the college you want. In this way, you took a short-term risk in pursuing a romantic relationship, but it can have negative long-term consequences that you don't want.

I see this battle play out in school all the time. You have to know what you want and what your commitment is to yourself. Are your goals intact, or are you getting distracted? This phenomenon is not confined to teenagers, either. I have compassion for what my students go through in their tumultuous romantic lives, because adults are just as affected and distracted by the uncertainty of dating, sex, and romance. No matter your age, it can be a huge letdown and a blow to your self-esteem if you let someone distract you from your life's goals, and then you break up and they're not in your life anymore.

IS THIS THE END OF FUN?

No! Of course it's not the end of fun. If you want to goof off, you can do so on a rare basis. Relaxation is absolutely necessary. You have to give your mind and body some down-time, because nobody can be focused and driven all the time—that's a great way to burn out, become overwhelmed and stressed, and even become sick. We don't want that. So, give yourself the breaks that you need, while still staying connected to the bigger picture. There's no need to be rigid. Life is here to enjoy, and it's fun to be spontaneous in the moment.

ENJOY THE PRESENT, EVEN AS YOU FOCUS ON THE FUTURE

Delaying gratification doesn't mean, "Well, I'm miserable right now, but I'm going to be happy in two years when I reach such-and-such goal." No. Goals are goals *because* they're a challenge to reach. Let's say you love running, and you've chosen to challenge yourself by competing in a marathon. No matter how passionate you are about running, there are going to be days that you don't want to get out of bed and get in that run. Maybe you don't feel well. Your muscles are sore. It's snowing outside. And yet you get out there and run—not because it's fun in the moment, but because you're looking forward to accomplishing your goal. When you get to marathon day, you feel strong and confident, and you're joined in community with thousands of other goal-setters who are likewise pushing themselves. It's a huge endorphin rush. You'll undoubtedly look back and think "Yep, all that training was worth it, even on the most difficult days."

So, you're not going to love the entire journey, but you can love most of it, especially if you've chosen a path you're passionate about. You can celebrate the small milestones along the way of reaching the big milestone. If you've been able to enjoy the journey, the destination feels good, but it's not absolutely everything. There's a balance between enjoying what you're doing and enjoying the outcome.

DO NOW! FIND A WAY TO STAY ENERGIZED TOWARD YOUR GOAL

Identify one of your long-term goals. What can you do today—and every day—to stay motivated toward reaching it. Perhaps you visualize the moment when you accomplish the goal. Maybe you set a daily calendar notification that pops up and reminds you what you're working toward. Maybe you craft a vision board or put a motivational image or phrase somewhere where you can see it—your screen saver, your bathroom mirror. Once one method loses its freshness, mix it up and try a different one.

YOUNG ADULTS TALK ABOUT...DELAYING GRATIFICATION

"I hate the way I feel when I don't meet a goal. I do it because I know I'll regret it later if I don't."

"I play baseball and I'm on a running program that I do three or four times a week. My dad checks in on me about it every day. If I don't do it, I just feel so bad, I can't even sleep. So I just do my thing right away when I get home."

"I have goals for high school, and what holds me accountable is my mom. She's my favorite person in the world and she grew up in a really poor family. The fact that she came from that, it makes me want to do well."

SHOW UP AND BE PRESENT

Have you ever looked around your classroom and noticed the kids who are sitting in their desks, but don't seem to *really* be present? Sure, they've got their butt in the seat, but their mind is elsewhere. They're sitting in the back of the class, checked out, sneaking around, playing with their phones. And this doesn't just happen at school—you'll see this on the job, with friends, and maybe even within your own family. There are a lot of people who, either literally or metaphorically, are sitting at the back of the classroom.

Education is the process of life. The whole world is a classroom. And if you spend your time "sitting at the back," you'll miss out on what life has to teach you.

Lessons present an opportunity for growth, and growth is one of the keys to happiness. Most of the time, the crucial lessons show up in the challenges we face. When I was in high school, I hated math. At points I was failing. A part of me was tempted to blame the teacher or the subject. But I had to be real with myself. Was I sitting at the front of the classroom, putting in my all? Truthfully, the answer was no—and I knew I had to make a change. If I was going to reach my goal of being the first in my family to graduate high school, I couldn't let math hold me back.

So I reached out for help. I sat at the front of the classroom, and I showed up after school for extra help. Instead of checking out and presuming I could never love math, I immersed myself in its study and cultivated personal relationships with my math teachers. Those teachers and I, we made an impact on each other because I sought their help and they enjoyed giving it. I thrived in the subject they taught, and I showed them gratitude (which is really all that most teachers want). I didn't just learn math—I learned to be accountable to my own growth, and to really show up and be present even during hard circumstances.

As a bonus: When you really show up with your full attention and presence, you create relationships with those around you, just like the give-and-take I cultivated with my high school math teachers. Those teachers even helped me with my math coursework when I went to college. These kinds of reciprocal relationships are incredible, and they're out there—with friends, family, teachers, and bosses. All you have to do is "sit at the front" and fully participate.

DO NOW! PROCESS A TOUGH CIRCUMSTANCE

Think about your life right now. Is there a situation—at school, work, or home—where you're "sitting at the back" instead of showing up and being fully present and engaged? Be honest with yourself. Next, take out your journal or a piece of paper and write about it:

- What's the tough situation?
- What isn't working in this situation?
- What are the positives?
- What are the possible solutions?

Once you've processed your thoughts in writing, approach whoever is it who can help you improve your situation. This could be a parent, teacher, coach, or supervisor. Advocate for yourself in a way that is respectful to you both, and co-create a solution that will allow you to shift your experience for the better.

WALK THE TALK

People like to talk. "I want to be famous." "I want to be rich." "I want to go to college." Okay, go ahead—do it! But...how? Don't just talk about what you want. Go after it. You've done the talking, and now it's time to do the walking.

Walking the talk has been a huge component of my own success. I could have dropped out of high school just like my parents did, but I chose to go to school. I could have been a haphazard athlete, but I chose to work as hard I could to get a full-ride scholarship. I could have chosen to party and use drugs or alcohol, but I didn't drink until I was twenty-four. I could have crumbled after I was sexually abused, but I used that as an opportunity to get strong, tough, and build my self-esteem.

No matter your circumstances or the hardships you face, when you set a goal, you are 100 percent within your power to go after it. This is an empowering place to be in. No matter where you're starting from, you can take steps to go after your dreams.

WALKING THE TALK IN ALL SIX FS

If you're going to be a healthy, whole person, you can't just walk the talk in one area of life. You have to have goals and accountability across all Six Fs: Future, Fitness, Friendships, Family, Finances, and Fun. If you spend too much time in one area, you'll neglect the others and won't become a well-rounded person. If you neglect your fitness in order to focus too much on fun, then you're ultimately harming yourself.

KEEP YOUR EYE ON THE BIG PICTURE

When things get hard, you can push through obstacles by focusing on the big picture of what's really driving you. Once your heart is connected to the big picture, you can zoom in your attention to break down your big picture into smaller, more manageable steps. For me, sports have always been a huge part of my life. When I was a high school basketball player, I needed to change my shooting technique. I accepted feedback from my basketball coach Terry Johnson and I agreed to practice on my own time. I followed the BEEF method: Balance, Eyes, Elbow, Follow-through. I watched an instructional video every single day. I practiced my shooting form every single day at Brooklyn Park. This was quality time with myself. And the payoff was great. Eventually I got it right, and my confidence on the court soared. And by honing my skills as an athlete, I opened up opportunities for myself—including a full scholarship to college. Nothing fuels self-love like thriving in an activity that you're passionate about.

MATCH YOUR EXTERNAL ACTIONS TO YOUR INTERNAL DIALOGUE

To really walk your talk, your internal dialogue needs to match up with your external actions, and this needs to happen consistently. You have to be accountable to your goals and personal commitments in your day-to-day habits. It has to be a daily practice—not weekly or monthly. You won't get what you want from life if you're only walking your talk once a month.

We all know people who are all talk, don't we? They set goals and talk about how great it would feel to achieve them, but they don't put any action into it. You don't build a reputation on what you're going to do, you build it on what you *have* done. So, when you're done "walking your talk," you get to "talk your walk." You get to say I DID IT. You get to prove to yourself and others that you have the skill and fortitude to create a big goal and then go after it until you're satisfied.

REAL EXPERIENCE PROVIDES REAL FEEDBACK

When you walk the talk, you actually get real-world practice, which gives you feedback. You want to be a rock star? Pick up the guitar. You hate it? Okay, that's feedback that maybe you don't want to be a rock star. Or maybe it's just feedback that you need to practice harder and not give up. The point is, you'll never know for sure until you get some real experience with your goals and see if the reality matches up to the fantasy.

YOUNG ADULTS TALK ABOUT...WALKING THEIR TALK

"I wanted to improve my range in high notes on my euphonium, and the thing that kept me going was setting more attainable goals—small ones, so at first it would be to hit F, and then step up until I've reached my entire range. It only took a few months. I came up with a regular routine, knew what I wanted, and set small and attainable goals."

"My goal for last track season was to get my 100 meter sprint to thirteen seconds. I broke thirteen and got 12.7 seconds. I really want to sprint in college, but my height has been an issue with that. Because I can't do long strides, I have to work harder. College motivates me."

DO NOW! CREATE A POSITIVE MANTRA

Mantras help you embody the positive mindset you're looking for. You can either make up your own mantra or take a famous quote that inspires you. One of my favorites is "I'm a first-rate person. Not a second-rate version of someone else." I keep this one in a frame right by my bedside. When you create or find a mantra that speaks to you, you can repeat it to yourself—either aloud or in your head—or you can create a visual representation and put it on your bathroom mirror, your bedroom wall, your binder, your journal, or as a screen saver on your phone or computer.

———————————————————

CONCLUSION

BEYOND THIS BOOK AND TO THE STARS

You've come to the end of this book, but you're just at the beginning of the rest of your life. If you've done the work up to this point, then you've given yourself some hands-on practice with ADANA Dynamics. Now it's up to you to take these skills beyond the page, to really own your destiny. Personal development is a lifelong process and doesn't stop until the day we die. Your life is your own personal masterpiece, and it can be as beautiful as you want, as long as you keep cultivating these skills: Acknowledge your current reality. Deal with it. Aspire. Have a no-nonsense attitude. Hold yourself accountable.

Of course, personal development isn't just about skills. At its core, it's about love. No matter how far you go in life, it all starts from the heart. When you fall in love with yourself, you become motivated from within and your natural goal-setting tendencies arise. Love is the rocket fuel that will propel you to the stars. You are a truly special person, with a wholly unique personality, perspective, and life experience. I want you to value and love yourself where you're at right now, and to also go confidently forward, knowing that you have access to the love and the tools to get you wherever you want to go.

Before you close the book, I want you to take some time for one last "Do Now" activity. Life is an active process, and there's always a positive step you can be taking right now.

DO NOW! TAKE SOME TIME FOR SELF-REFLECTION

Create a quiet environment where you can be alone. Turn off your phone and computer and tablet, and make sure you're free of all distractions. Now, take out your journal and reflect on how far you've come through the ADANA Dynamics process. Try to really step back and observe yourself without bias. Ask yourself: Are you healthy? Do you feel like you are taking care of you? Do you feel like you are taking 100 percent accountability for your life? How is your self-esteem, and what can you do to improve it? If there are areas where you're excelling, take a moment to focus on the good and celebrate it. If there are areas where you need improvement, make a plan for doing so.

AN INVITATION TO SHARE YOUR STORY...

When we share our stories together, we create the human connection that we all crave. I'm touched and inspired by all of the people in my life, and I love hearing their personal stories of hardship and triumph. That's why I'm thrilled to announce that the next project from ADANA Dynamics is a collection of letters and stories written by you, the readers. Whether you're a young adult or a parent, guardian, teacher, coach, or role model, I want to hear about how you've used ADANA Dynamics to change your life for the better.

Visit me online at **www.adanadynamics.com** to learn more about the next project and to submit your own stories.

DO NOW! THE COMPLETE CHECKLIST

You've read *Motivate from Within* and tried the "Do Now" activities—*but don't stop there*. The Do Now's are designed to be relevant and revealing at any time of life. Revisit the exercises often. You'll be sure to gain something new every time.

- ❑ Meditate to Discover Your Feelings (page 4)
- ❑ Free Write to Discover Your Feelings (page 6)
- ❑ Write Yourself a Love Letter (page 9)
- ❑ Look in the Mirror (page 15)
- ❑ Analyze Your Influences (page 22)
- ❑ Write a Gratitude Letter to a Positive Influence (page 22)
- ❑ Write an "I See You" Letter (page 26)
- ❑ See the Good in the People Around You (page 29)
- ❑ Relax into the Present (page 35)
- ❑ Make a Pros and Cons Chart to Face a Hard Reality (page 43)
- ❑ Observe Your Feelings (page 45)
- ❑ Make Time to Connect (page 47)
- ❑ Write a "Thank You" Letter to a Supporter (page 48)
- ❑ Let It Go (page 50)
- ❑ Create a Physical Symbol of Your Problem...and Then Destroy It (page 50)
- ❑ Process Your Family Hardship in a Journal (page 52)
- ❑ Create an Endurance Challenge (page 54)
- ❑ Give It 100 Days (page 60)
- ❑ Play! (page 60)
- ❑ Browse the Self-Help Section (page 66)
- ❑ Tally Your Gadget Use (page 69)
- ❑ Have a Gadget-Free Table Talk (page 69)
- ❑ Identify Healthy Coping Strategies (page 74)

❑ Write a Letter from Your Future Self (page 75)
❑ Think of a Time When You Were Most Happy (page 80)
❑ Make a List of Personal Commitments (page 81)
❑ Chart the 24 Hours of Your Day (page 82)
❑ Create 101 Wishes (page 88)
❑ Revisit a Past Goal (page 89)
❑ Create Long-Term and Short-Term Goals (page 89)
❑ Have a Table Talk on Goal Setting (page 90)
❑ Create a Vision Board (page 95)
❑ Write a "Thank You" Letter to Your Mentor or Role Model (page 100)
❑ Find an Activity Buddy (page 107)
❑ Craft a Goal-Setting Card (page 108)
❑ Journal about the Quality People in Your Life (page 109)
❑ Write a Love Letter to a Quality Person in Your Life (page 109)
❑ Create Ten Commitments (page 114)
❑ E + R = O (page 114)
❑ Surround Yourself with Inspiration (page 118)
❑ Take in the Good (page 118)
❑ See Yourself in the Future (page 119)
❑ Free Write Your Reactions (page 125)
❑ Dissipate the Energy (page 125)
❑ Reflect on Feedback You've Received (page 125)
❑ Reflect on Accountability Partners (page 132)
❑ Find a Way to Stay Energized toward Your Goal (page 136)
❑ Process a Tough Circumstance (page 140)
❑ Create a Positive Mantra (page 143)
❑ Take Some Time for Self-Reflection (page 146)

SOURCES

Canfield, Jack, and Mark Victor Hansen. *Dare to Win*. New York:
   Berkley, 1996.

Canfield, Jack, and Janet Switzer. *The Success Principles: How to
   Get from Where You Are to Where You Want to Be*. New York:
   Collins, 2005.

Hanson, Rick. *Wired for Happiness: The New Brain Science of
   Contentment, Calm, and Confidence*. New York: Harmony, 2013.

Hawkins, David R. *Letting Go: The Pathway of Surrender*. Carlsbad,
   CA: Hay House, 2014.

Tolle, Eckhart. *The Power of Now: A Guide to Spiritual Enlightenment*.
   Vancouver, BC: Namaste, 2004.

"Why Teens Are Impulsive, Addiction-Prone and Should Protect
   Their Brains." NPR *Fresh Air*, January 28, 2015: http://www.npr.
   org/blogs/health/2015/01/28/381622350/why-teens-are-impulsive-
   addiction-prone-and-should-protect-their-brains.

ACKNOWLEDGMENTS

Let me start by expressing how much I appreciate the patience and support of every significant person in my life who took the time to listen to me dream about becoming an author and a success coach. I'm grateful for the family, friends, students, and even strangers who have sincerely listened and provided genuine support as I was walking my talk. The journey of creating this book has taken seven years and has gone through many phases. My heart is touched by all the people who kept the faith all this time.

It all began when I received a volleyball that was dedicated to me and signed by **Linda McLellan**, my role model in high school. Linda was my volleyball coach and health/physical education teacher, and after earning my undergraduate degree at Concordia University in Portland, Oregon, she gave me a volleyball inscribed with a message: "You will achieve and make all your dreams come true." This gift reminded me that achieving dreams can continue on and not just be based in high school or college goals. The signed, dedicated volleyball opened my eyes and started my process of creating bigger visions for the future. I am so thankful for you, Linda, for believing in my motivation and always empowering me to be a strong woman and to never give up.

I am so truly thankful for **Jan Watt**, who has played many roles in my life. Jan, you were my mentor and teacher in high school. I remember loving your candid approach to teaching and your no-enabling approach in the classroom. I remember taking a mental note and writing in my journal about how I wanted to be like you when I grew up. Sure enough, I get to Cleveland and feel like I have a little bit of you in me. I have been blessed to work with you on a daily basis and I couldn't be more thankful. We "get" each other, and for this I want you to know how much you mean to me. Nothing compares to working with you! You are not only my mentor and role model, you are my friend and a part of my family. You will always be the strength that I need to get through any and all adversity.

I am also sincerely grateful for **Craig Montag**, my first positive male role model. I appreciate you, Craig, for having expectations, guidelines, and rules, and for being a person who constantly gave feedback. I will always treasure the days when I was a park director with you at Brooklyn Park. Our dual approach impacted kids immensely and the experience made us even closer. Our bond is very significant and I have no idea where I would be without you. I am truly thankful for you, Craig. You've taught me to be true to myself and how to make an impact.

Gaye Chapman, you are my teaching partner and great friend. I have so much respect for what you teach me on a day-to-day basis. Your beautiful, calming, nonjudgmental soul gets me through every working day at Cleveland High School. Thank you for constantly challenging me as a professional and, most of all, for being the best listener I know. Your unconditional love and support have shaped my life.

Kendra Gardner, my friend, teaching comrade, and accountability coach. We have always had the best connection around setting goals and following through. I appreciate the way you always look forward and think big, and I admire your ability to walk your talk. You have accomplished every dream you have set forth to accomplish. Your leadership and modeling have been pivotal in my growth as a professional and as a goal-setter, and with actually following through. I truly appreciate our conversations, our walks, and our laughter.

To my **health and leadership students** who embrace my teaching philosophy and animated approach, thank you for accepting my uniqueness and passion to motivate. I am a very "in your face" and candid communicator, as well as an open book, and you all have accepted me. Thank you, Cleveland Warriors, for embracing my energy and for believing in my future aspirations.

Thank you to all the **athletes** I have had the honor to coach. You have taught me the true meaning of goal-setting and follow-through. I have had the most amazing seasons that a coach could ever ask for, and it was only because my athletes, in every given situation or sport, tried their best on a day-to-day basis. I am so proud of all of you young women who chose to work hard on the court, on the field, in the classroom, and in life. Your choices to walk your talk truly empowered me to continue going after my dreams. Thank you, ladies!

Thank you, **Cleveland High School staff members**. I know that may seem general, but I would have to write another book to share my gratitude about all of you people! I have amazing, insightful, challenging, supportive conversations every day in this beautiful profession. Thank you for opening your heart to my passion project, *Motivate from Within*.

Extra shout-out to **Violet Trachtenberg** for putting extra effort into my journey. Violet spent countless hours donating her time reading and giving feedback. Violet was a student of mine at Cleveland High School who graduated at the top of her class and moved on to Stanford University. Thank you, Violet, for being amazing and extending your mind to help me do my best.

To **Kristi Lee Fowlks**, who started a GoFundMe campaign without my knowing and encouraging her friends to support me in funding the writing and publishing of *Motivate from Within*. Kristi, who graduated from Cleveland High School in 2003, was my very first student body president. She has a spirit about her that is vibrant and inspirational. Thank you, Kristi, for believing in me and for adding sunshine to my life with your smile and powerful insights.

Thank you to **Sheila Ashdown** for being a professional, a great listener, and a wonderful writer. You supported me, believed in me and ADANA Dynamics, understood my desire to motivate, and embraced my candid approach. Sheila, you will forever be a business partner, my friend, and truly a part of my family.

Thank you to my photographer and friend **Angie Tabaczynski**, who gave her heart and passion to the process of creating photographs for the book and website. Thank you, Angie, for volunteering your time and skill and for having faith in me.

Oprah Winfrey, you are my go-to person. You have been my rock. I need to hear your voice because you soothe my soul. I love you more than words can express, and I believe in my heart that I'll meet you someday and get the opportunity to hug you tightly. Thank you, Oprah, for saving my life.

Jack Canfield, your existence matters more than I know how to express. Your desire to make an impact has taught me how to walk my talk and accomplish any and all of my dreams.

Ellen DeGeneres, the way you make me laugh has taught me to live in the moment. I feel like your determination to be successful after going through so much hardship has been a huge inspiration in my life.

This project could not have been accomplished without financial support of **generous donors**. Thank you so very much to all who took the time to donate and show your faith in me as an author and inspiration. I am blessed to have all of you in my life, and I appreciate you opening up your wallets to support my dream. The people below are friends, family, current and former students and their parents, and kind strangers who read about the project and felt compelled to donate. Thank you for using PubSlush, GoFundMe, sending checks, and/or hand delivering money to support the writing and publication of *Motivate from Within*:

Jocelyn Kragero, Sabrina Blue and David Blue, Eric Levine, Letisha King, Robert Adana, Josie and Nate Boccuzzi-Hall, Rick and Norma King, Vanessa Hughes, Peter Schulert, Kendra Gardner, Mara Barnes, Dan Drullinger, Gail Adams, Dona Dumdeang, Lynne Gardner-Allers, Katrina Sonniksen, Rena Shuman, Tessa Ryan, Angie Tabaczynski, Nancy Fox, Rachel Fox and Emma Fox, Kennedy Wolfe, Mackenzie Wolfe, Loreen Nichols, Hilary Nichols, Coni Ingram, Maia Hamilton, Sara Kane, Lora Giles, Gaye Chapman, Michael Schmeer, Sally (Aunt Sissy) Thomas, Jamyang Dorjee, Brenda Gordon, Hao Nguyen, Allison Wilson, Bella Forrest, Hannah Baggao, Nadia Aazad, Pearl Barnes, Cassandra O'Hearn, Gary and Jessica Hedges, Brian Brown, Thom and Jane Bray, Corriedawn Greiling, Trisha Olson, Travis Siems, Alex

Souther, Cory Woods, Dori Smith, Brenda Sutton, Sarah Gredvig, Rebecca Amy, Kathryn Arnone, Linda McLellan, Patricia King and Noble Herricks, Nghia Ho, Melissa Iwamoto, Benjamin Rosen, Keri Dehen, Renee Dehen, Sheila Ashdown, DeVan Whitaker, Angela Hemming and Ryan Hemming, Howard Lao, Karen and John Hoke, Michelle Hawkins, Nnamdi Agum, Jodee and Geoff Smith, Richard Breece, Kristi Lee Fowlks and personal friends of Kristi Fowlks, Ashley McIntyre, Don and Kristi Hopkins, Mike and Katie Shanahan, Julia Kohn-Brown, Amie Teller, Cory Hedges, and those donors who asked to remain anonymous. Thank you all so very much.

Mom, I wouldn't be who I am if I didn't have your unconditional love and support from day one. You have always been by my side and given me the freedom to find myself. You have never judged me and you are the best listener a daughter could ever have. I appreciate you opening your heart when I have needed to cry, feel, vent, or simply just to talk. You are my rock, my inspiration, and my best friend. I love you, mama.

Robert Adana, my baby brother, you have been such a lover in my life. You have a way with words when you get fired up! I appreciate you believing in me always. You have never lost faith in me in any way. You were by my side at every sporting event when I was in high school. You've always allowed me to cry on your shoulder when I needed to, and you've always been the person to bring laughter to my very intense days. Your sense of humor and love for me has shown immensely and I just want to say thank you for having enthusiasm about my dream and spreading it to the world

Thank you to my sister, **Pearl Barnes**, who always answers the phone when I call. You are always a phone call away and you give me your listening ear and constant support no matter what you are in the middle of doing. This book has taken many forms and gone through many different drafts, and you have been right by my side throughout. You are encouraging and so very attentive. I have appreciated being able to read to you and get your honest feedback. I am so thankful you allowed me to use you as an example to motivate the future. What I appreciate the most about you is that you are walking the talk of ADANA Dynamics every day of your life. You are trying your best to be the best, and you don't give up on learning. Thank you for allowing me to inspire you, but most of all for giving me your heart always.

Thank you, **Auntie Gail Adams**, for stretching my imagination, for helping me visualize beyond my current reality or circumstances. You've taught me to think outside the box and to not be afraid to be alone. Your modeling of strength, determination, curiosity, and individuality has truly made an impact. I hope you know how much I appreciate and love you, my sweet auntie Gail.

To my aunties, **Gwen Friese**, **Marie Young**, **Rachel Iwamoto**, and **Jude Woods**. You all brought so much love and support to my life. I will always remember the time, money, and energy you put into our family to feed us, clothe us, and support our tumultuousness when I was a young girl. Thank you for coming together often and showing me the beauty of conversation, music, dance, love, and laughter.

Uncle Peter Darling, I don't see you very often, but I want you to know that the many conversations we had revealed to me your potential and what kind of heart you have. Thank you for making an impact on my life during the intermittent moments we've had together.

Sabrina Blue and **Melissa Iwamoto**, I want to thank you both for being the light of my life. Your vibrant, genuine laughter and smiles help get me past all obstacles. Even though we've all experienced similar dynamics in our lives, you both choose to see the best in every situation. You both have such skill in choosing optimism. I sincerely appreciate you both so very much.

Cory and Cameron Woods, I care about you both. We have a wonderful relationship even though a lot of time goes by without seeing each other. Our relationship is filled with support, laughter, and family memories. Thank you both for being major supporters and believing in me.

Nicole Narong, your constant determination to be the best has been a strong motivator for me. I have always felt you were a quiet leader and amazing at what you do always. Remembering when you are born and what you have become has been an outstanding example of a person I respect. I hope you know how proud I am of you. Thank you sincerely for being a huge support.

Aaron Adana, thank you for treasuring me, listening to me, believing in me, and pushing me toward greatness. I am so happy you found us, and I'm looking forward to our many years ahead.

Josie Boccuzzi-Hall, we met at Cleveland High School and have been best friends ever since. We don't change at all when we're together. We have inside jokes, we're crazy together, we can chill together, we love preparing and eating food together. We never fight, our love is unconditional, we are family, and nothing will ever break us apart. What I appreciate the most is your support and how you show your love to me. Thank you, Josie, for being consistent and embracing me as family.

Nate Hall, Angie Hemming, Ryan Hemming, Apollonia Boccuzzi, Anna Boccuzzi, and **Mom and Dad Boccuzzi:** You've provided the deep love, laughter, and support I needed to get through difficult times. I have enjoyed all of our conversations, family get-togethers, vacations, food, and inside jokes. I've loved and appreciated every minute we've spent together and look forward to much more time together in our future.

Thank you to **Donice Villanova** for always asking how I'm doing and caring about me as person. Your heart is visible and I appreciate you immensely.

Mekeala Hemming, you have always been my sidekick! Thank you for all of our interactions and for feeling comfortable talking to me about life. I have truly enjoyed our deep conversations, laughter, and of course our coaching experience together. There is nothing like the Mekeala/Camille duo! Our energy is very similar and I will always treasure us.

AJ Hemming, "wise beyond your years" is what I think when I think about you. I respect your intelligence, potential, and charismatic approach to life. You should have the same birthday as me—if only your mom could have waited one more hour! I hope you know how much you mean to me, AJ. Keep going strong and continue being determined to be a success.

Enza and Ruby Boccuzzi-Hall, the future is ahead and there is so much for the both of you to look forward too. Your personalities and smarts will take you both so very far. I hope you know Auntie Mille Mille will always be a listening ear and a supporter while you go through this wonderful life.

Noah and Kylee Barnes, keep being amazing and go after your dreams. Your Auntie Mille Mille will always be by your side. I love you both so very much and hope you realize what you are capable of accomplishing from within. Please believe in you and go after your heart's desires.

Preslei Ann Adana, keep being the strong, loving young woman you are. You bring laughter and joy into my life. I look forward to our memories ahead. Miss you.

Eva and Kai Adana, time keeps moving and we do not get much time to chat or spend together, but don't ever forget you are an Adana and I love you both very much. I also look forward to the future ahead. Believe in yourself and keep your head up.

To my grandma **Clarabel Smith:** Thank you, Grandma, for sharing your wisdom, optimistic attitude, and chill approach to life. You taught me how to live in the moment and how to laugh. You singing to me during your last days will forever be etched in my heart. "Don't Worry, Be Happy." I love you, Grandma.

To my dad, **Robert Allen Adana Sr.:** I promised you I would write a book and that I would share you within the book. You are a difficult person to describe, but what I know about you the most is that you did the best you could as a father. I feel you left too soon, but, at the same time, your passing on taught our family to stay together and to never take a day for granted. We have maintained our love and devotion to each other and I believe it is because we lost you. I know you are in a better place and definitely more content. I love you, we love you, and you will never be forgotten.

ABOUT THE AUTHORS

Camille Adana has been inspiring teens and young adults for 16 years (and counting) as a coach and teacher of health and leadership at Cleveland High School in Portland, Oregon. She is also the creator of ADANA Dynamics, a five-step process that inspires people of all ages and stages of life to set goals and achieve their dreams. Camille holds a BA in Physical and Health Education, with a teaching certificate, from Concordia University in Portland, Oregon; a BS in Health and Fitness Promotions from Portland State University; and a Masters in Curriculum and Instruction, Secondary Education, from Concordia University. Camille played college basketball and softball at Concordia University and finished her career playing Division 1 softball at Portland State University. Visit Camille online at www.adanadynamics.com.

Sheila Ashdown is a freelance writer and editor, dedicated to helping authors write and publish books that inspire and inform. Find her online at www.sheilaashdown.com.